Charlie D. Tillman

Revival, No. 2

Suitable for all kinds of religious meetings.

Charlie D. Tillman

Revival, No. 2
Suitable for all kinds of religious meetings.

ISBN/EAN: 9783337719487

Printed in Europe, USA, Canada, Australia, Japan

Cover: Foto ©Lupo / pixelio.de

More available books at **www.hansebooks.com**

Yes, We Understand

All about how you are bothered to keep your book open on your Piano or Organ, and you can overcome all this by the use of the

... THE BARTLEY ...
OPEN BOOK HOLDER.

✤✤ PRICES. ✤✤

Nickeled Wire,	15c., or 2 for 25c.
Smooth Nickel,	each, $0 25
Aluminum,	" .50
Silver,	" 1 60
Silver Ornamented,	" 2 00
Gold-plated,	" 3 00
Solid Gold,	" 15 00

ADDRESS ALL ORDERS TO

CHARLIE D. TILLMAN,

Atlanta, Ga.   Cincinnati, O.   Kansas City, Mo.

Motion Songs.		Sweet Songs.
Bright Songs.		Beautiful Songs.
Easy Songs.		"Singable" Songs.
"Catchy" Songs.		Living Songs.

These are reduced pages from "Little Light."

The little folks WANT to sing. Get this book of songs which they CAN sing.
SAMPLE COPY TEN CENTS.

SAM JONES' OPINION

of THE REVIVAL No. 2 after using it in the great Jones & Stuart Atlanta meeting in which over two thousand copies were sold:

"These songs go and they carry the people with them Gospel principles and power, music and melody combined I know of no better song book extant."

SAM P. JONES.

March, 1896.

See 190-194

The Revival No. 2.

No. 3.   EVER BE FAITHFUL.

E. A. H.
Rev. E. A. HOFFMAN.

1. Ev-er to Je-sus be faith-ful and true, He has been ten-der and faith-ful to you; Fol-low Him dai-ly what-ev-er be-tide, Fol-low your Lead-er and Guide.
2. Hon-or the Mas-ter by do-ing His will, Love Him, and all His com-mandments ful-fill; And as you jour-ney life's pilgrimage through, Ev-er be faith-ful and true.
3. Cling un-to Je-sus, thy Strength and thy Might, Cling in the darkness, and cling in the light, Hon-or His name in what-ev-er you do, Ev-er be faith-ful and true.

CHORUS.

Ev - - er be faith - ful, Ev - - er be faith - ful, Ev - - er be faith - ful, Ev - er be true.
ev-er be true, Ev-er be faithful, and ev-er be true, He has been tender and faithful to you, Ev-er be faithful and true.

By per. J. H. Kurzenknabe, owner of copyright.

THE JUDGMENT. Concluded.

said with his hand raised to heaven, That time was no long-er to
an - gel that o-pened the rec - ords, Not a trace of his greatness could
peo - ple who gave him the li - cense—To - geth-er in hell they did
time now to think of re - lig - ion!" At last they had found time to

be.
find. And oh, what a weep-ing and wail-ing When the
sink.
die.

lost ones were told of their fate; They cried for the

rocks and the moun-tains, They prayed, but their pray'rs were too late

No. 7. SCATTER SUNSHINE.

LANTA WILSON SMITH. E. O. EXCELL.

1. In a world where sor-row Ev-er will be known, Where are found the need-y, And the sad and lone; How much joy and com-fort You can all be-stow, If you scatter sunshine Ev'rywhere you go.
2. Slightest actions oft-en Meet the sor-est needs, For the world wants dai-ly, Lit-tle kind-ly deeds; Oh, what care and sor-row, You may help remove, With your songs and courage, Sym-pa-thy and love.
3. When the days are gloomy, Sing some happy song, Meet the world's re-pin-ing, With a cour-age strong; Go with faith un-daunt-ed, Thro' the ills of life, Scatter smiles and sunshine, O'er its toil and strife.

CHORUS.

Scat - - ter sunshine all a-long your way, . . Cheer and bless and bright-en Ev-'ry pass-ing day, . . Ev-'ry pass-ing day.
Scatter the smiles and o-ver the way,

Copyright, 1892, by E. O. Excell.

No. 8. Steer Straight to the Light-House.

T. W. D.
T. W. DENNINGTON.

1. Say where are you go-ing, my broth-er, Up-on the broad o-cean of time? Are you bound for the land of the bless-ed, A home in fair Canaan's bright clime?
2. Be sure that the Sav-iour is with thee Where-ev-er thy life boat may go, Should you take your life journey without Him, You'll sink 'neath the billows of woe.
3. Look not on the lamps that burn dim-ly; But look to the light of God's love: Look not on the wrecks by the sea-shore, But look to the light-house a-bove.

CHORUS.

Steer straight to the light-house, my broth-er, There's dan-ger up-on the dark wave, Ask Je-sus to keep and to guide you. He's a-ble and will-ing to save.

Copyright, 1895, by Charlie D. Tillman.

ONLY A DRUNKARD. Concluded.

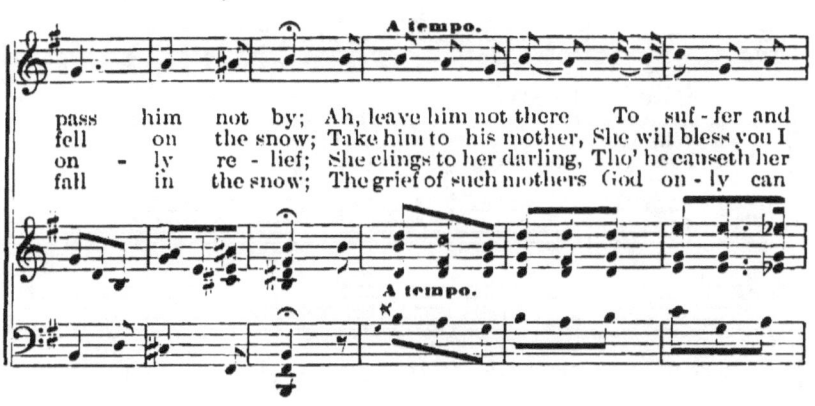

pass him not by; Ah, leave him not there To suf-fer and
fell on the snow; Take him to his mother, She will bless you I
on - ly re - lief; She clings to her darling, Tho' he causeth her
fall in the snow; The grief of such mothers God on - ly can

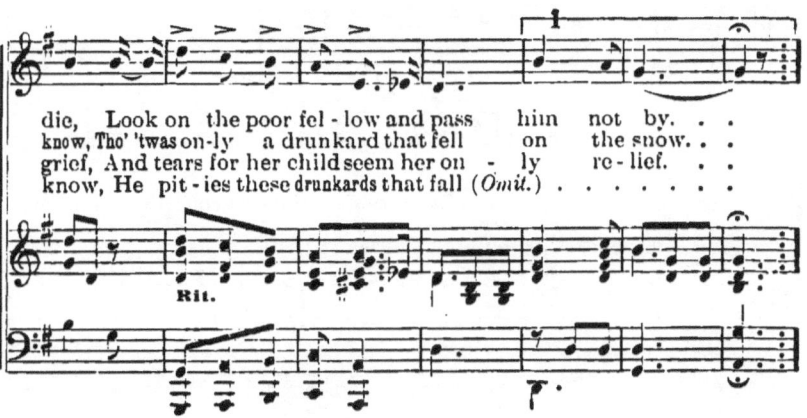

die, Look on the poor fel - low and pass him not by. . .
know, Tho' 'twas on-ly a drunkard that fell on the snow. . .
grief, And tears for her child seem her on - ly re - lief. . .
know, He pit - ies these drunkards that fall (*Omit.*) . . . . .

in the snow. . . . .

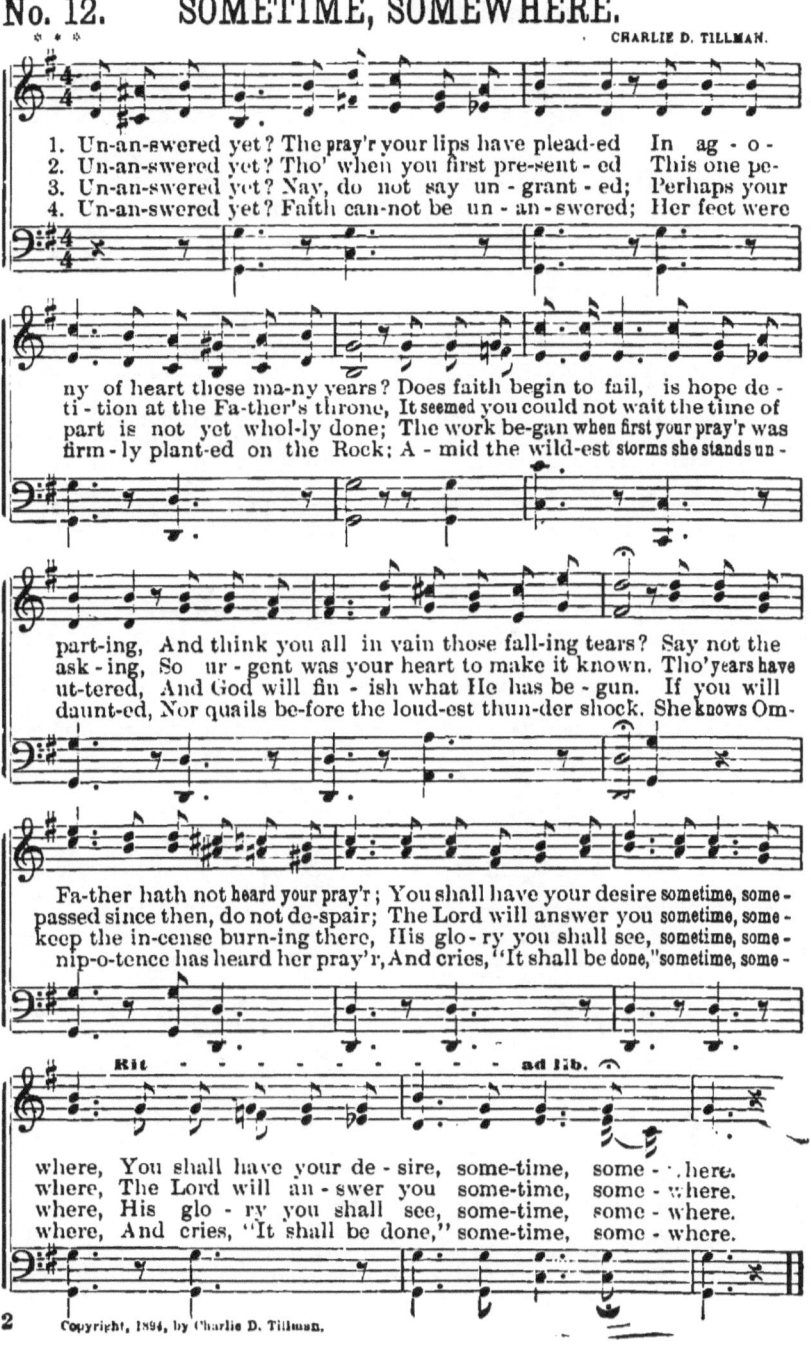

MARCHING TO VICTORY. Concluded.

way, For our Captain gone before bids us nev-er be dismay'd,

He assures us vic-t'ry shall not be de-layed. . . . .
not be delayed.

No. 14.   I CAN, I WILL.

1. Re-fin-ing fire, go thro' my heart, Re-fin-ing fire, go thro' my heart.
2. Scat-ter thy life thro' ev-ry part, Scat-ter thy life thro' ev'ry part,
3. Oh, that it now from heav'n might fall, Oh, that it now from heav'n might fall
4. Come, Ho-ly Ghost, for Thee I call, Come, Holy Ghost, for Thee I call,

Cho. No. 1. I can, I will, I do be-lieve, I can, I will, I do believe,
Cho. No. 2. I'm kneeling at the mer-cy seat, I'm kneeling at the mercy seat,

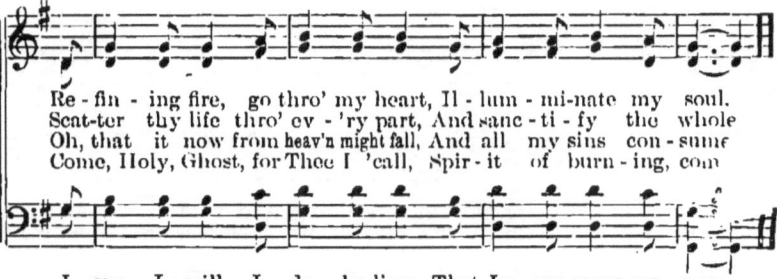

Re-fin-ing fire, go thro' my heart, Il-lum-mi-nate my soul.
Scat-ter thy life thro' ev-'ry part, And sanc-ti-fy the whole
Oh, that it now from heav'n might fall, And all my sins con-sume
Come, Holy, Ghost, for Thee I 'call, Spir-it of burn-ing, com

I can, I will, I do be-lieve, That Je-sus saves me now.
I'm kneeling at the mer-cy seat, Where Je-sus an-swers pray'r.

BRIGHTER AND BRIGHTER. Concluded.

sweet - - ly I rest . . in His love, (in His love.)
rest in His love, And more and more sweetly I rest in His love.

No. 16. DOWN AT CALVARY'S FOUNTAIN.

L. E. J. L. E. JONES.

1. I'm redeem'd and washed from sin, Down at Cal-v'ry's foun-tain,
2. Joy I find be-yond compare, Down at Cal-v'ry's foun-tain,
3. Bur-dens great are rolled a-way, Down at Cal-v'ry's foun-tain,
4. Per-fect peace the Lord has giv'n, Down at Cal-v'ry's foun-tain,

There the cleans-ing tide comes in, Down at Cal-v'ry's foun-tain.
Je-sus comes and meets me there, Down at Cal-v'ry's foun-tain.
Strife with self all ceased for aye, Down at Cal-v'ry's foun-tain.
Peace and rest like that of heav'n, Down at Cal-v'ry's foun-tain.

CHORUS.

There is cleans-ing in the tide As it flows from Calv'ry's side,
To my heart it is ap-plied, Down at Cal-v'ry's foun-tain.

Copyright, 1895, by Charlie D Tillman.

THE HEALED PINION. Concluded.

I WILL SHOUT HIS PRAISE. Concluded.

glo-ry, . . . And we'll all sing hal-le-lu-jah in heaven by and by.
So will I, so will I,

No. 19.   **TAKE ME AS I AM.**

From "The Garner," by per.

Melody by J. H. STOCKTON.
Har. by W. J. K.

1. Je-sus, my Lord, to Thee I cry, Un-less Thou help me I must die;
2. Help-less I am, and full of guilt, But yet for me Thy blood was spilt,
3. No prep-a-ra-tion can I make, My best re-solves I on-ly break,
4. I thirst, I long to know Thy love, Thy full sal-va-tion I would prove;

Oh, bring Thy free sal-va-tion nigh, And take me as I am!
And Thou canst make me what Thou wilt, But take me as I am!
Yet save me for Thine own name's sake, And take me as I am!
But since to Thee I can-not move, Oh, take me as I am!

D.S. bring Thy free sal-va-tion nigh, And take me as I am!

REFRAIN.

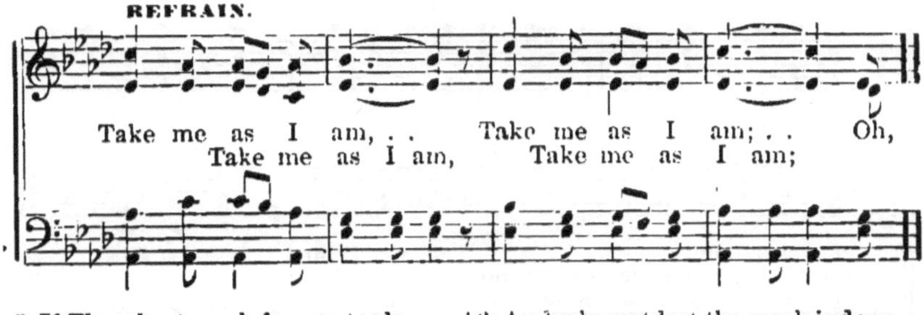

Take me as I am, .. Take me as I am; .. Oh,
Take me as I am, Take me as I am;

5 If Thou hast work for me to do,
Inspire my will, my heart renew,
And work both in and by me too,
But take me as I am!

6 And when at last the work is done,
The battle o'er, the vict'ry won,
Still, still my cry shall be alone,
Lord, take me as I am!

No. 24. FILL ME NOW.

E. H. STOKES, D. D.   JNO. R. SWENEY.

1. Hov - er o'er me, Ho - ly Spir-it, Bathe my trembling heart and brow;
2. Thou canst fill me, gracious Spirit, Tho' I can - not tell Thee how;
3. I am weakness, full of weakness, At Thy sa-cred feet I bow;
4. Cleanse and comfort, bless and save me; Bathe, oh, bathe my heart and brow;

Fill me with Thy hallowed presence, Come, oh, come and fill me now.
But I need Thee, greatly need Thee, Come, oh, come and fill me now.
Blest, divine, e - ter - nal Spir - it, Fill with pow'r and fill me now.
Thou art com-fort-ing and sav - ing, Thou art sweetly fill- ing now.

D. S. Fill me with Thy hallowed presence, Come, oh, come, and fill me now.

CHORUS.

Fill me now, fill me now, Je - sus come and fill me now.

Copyright, 1879, by John J. Hood. Used by per.

No. 25. THE BEAUTIFUL RIVER.

1 Shall we gather at the river
  Where bright angel feet have trod;
With its crystal tide forever
  Flowing by the throne of God?

Cho.—Yes, we'll gather at the river,
  The beautiful, the beautiful river—
Gather with the saints at the river,
  That flows by the throne of God.

2 On the margin of the river,
  Washing up its silver spray,
We will walk and worship ever,
  All the happy golden day.

3 Ere we reach the shining river,
  Lay we every burden down;
Grace our spirits will deliver,
  And provide a robe and crown.

4 Soon we'll reach the silver river,
  Soon our pilgrimage will cease;
Soon our happy hearts will quiver
  With the melody of peace.

ROBERT LOWRY.

No. 27. DIAMONDS IN THE ROUGH.

CHARLIE D. TILLMAN.

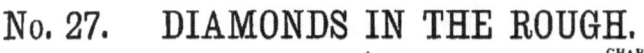

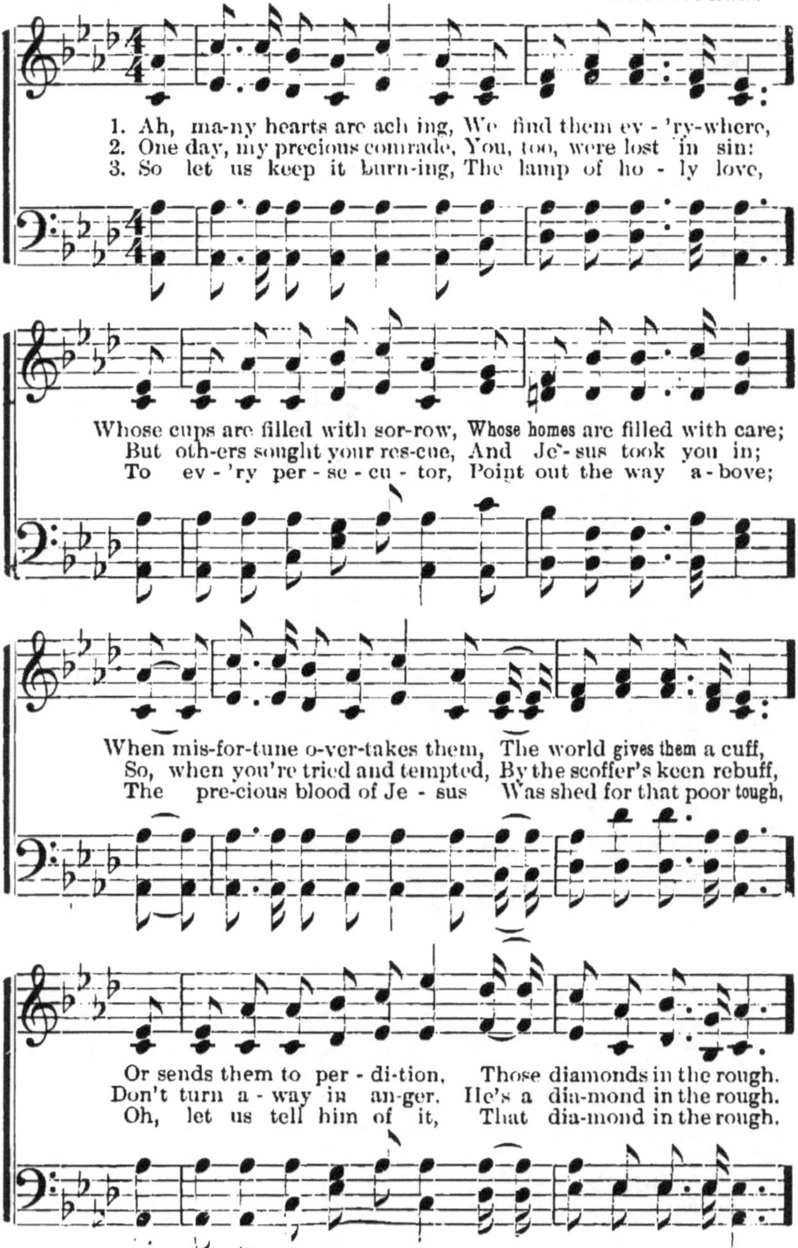

DIAMONDS IN THE ROUGH. Concluded.

No. 28. When I Get to the End of the Way.

CHARLIE D. TILLMAN.

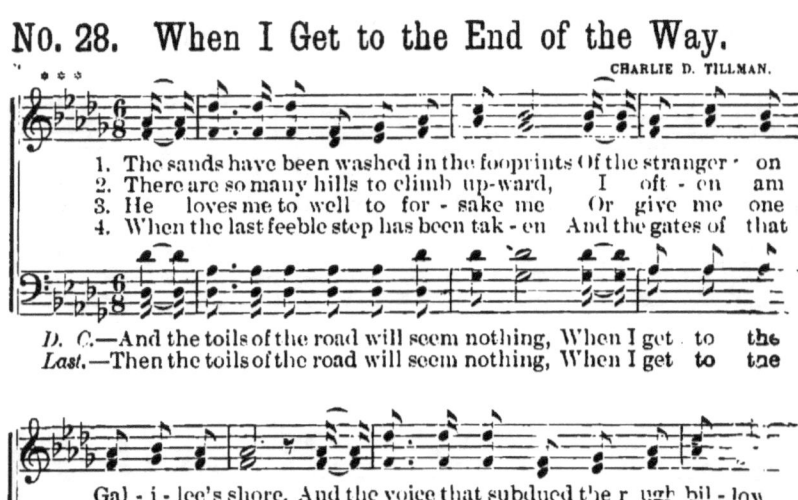

1. The sands have been washed in the footprints Of the stranger on Gal-i-lee's shore, And the voice that subdued the rough bil-low
2. There are so many hills to climb up-ward, I oft-en am longing for rest, But He who ap-points me my pathway,
3. He loves me too well to for-sake me Or give me one tri-al too much, All His peo-ple have been dear-ly purchased,
4. When the last feeble step has been tak-en And the gates of that cit-y ap-pear And the beau-ti-ful songs of the an-gels

D. C.—And the toils of the road will seem nothing, When I get to the end of the way, And the toils of the road will seem nothing,
Last.—Then the toils of the road will seem nothing, When I get to the end of the way, Then the toils of the road will seem nothing,

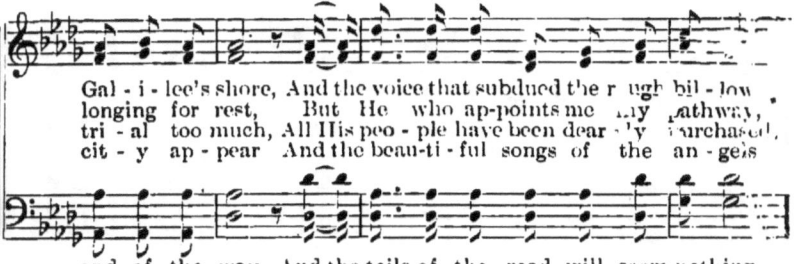

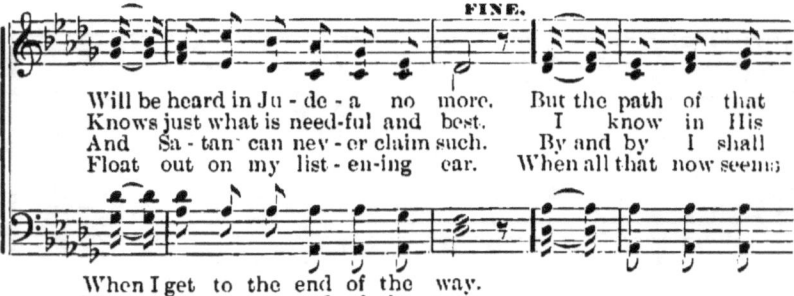

Will be heard in Ju-de-a no more. But the path of that lone Gal-i-lee-an With joy I will fol-low to-day.
Knows just what is need-ful and best. I know in His word He hath promised That my strength, "it shall be as my day."
And Sa-tan can nev-er claim such. By and by I shall see Him and praise Him, In the cit-y of un-end-ing day.
Float out on my list-en-ing ear. When all that now seems so mys-te-ri-ous Will be bright and as clear as the day.

When I get to the end of the way.
When I get to the end of the way.

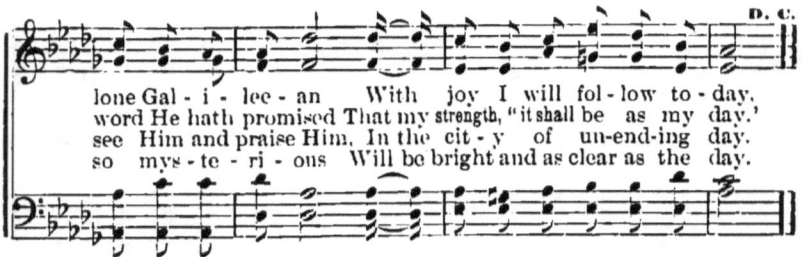

Copyright, 1895, by Charlie D. Tillman.

No. 31. SINCE TO MY HEART JESUS CAME.

L. E. J.   L. E. JONES.

1. I have been saved from the pow'r of sin; Since to my
2. Rest I have found from the cares of life, Since to my
3. Things of this world I de - sire no more, Since to my
4. I am led safe - ly from day to day, Since to my

heart Je - sus came, Washed at the fount-ain made white and clean,
heart Je - sus came, Par - don and peace, af - ter wea - ry strife,
heart Je - sus came, Bur - dens are lift - ed that once I bore;
heart Je - sus came, Glad - ly I walk in the nar - row way,

Since to my heart Je - sus came.

CHORUS.

Earth is so fair, and the sky is so bright, Troubles are scat-tered and toil seems so light; Safe-ly I'm kept thro' His love and His might, Since to my heart Je-sus came.

Copyright, 1895, by Charlie D. Tillman.

No. 34. LEAVE IT TO HIM.

J. E. RANKIN. CHAS. H. GABRIEL.

1. Why go around with troubled soul? There's One that makes the wounded whole;
2. How-ev-er man thy lot may slight, He'll turn to day thy darkest night,
3. How-ev-er dark thy path may be, Dark and un-scru-ta-ble to thee,
4. Sure He who sets the mountain fast, When all earth's clouds are driven past,

Up - on the Lord thy burden roll;—Leave it to Him, leave it to
And flood from heav'n thy path with light,
He rules on high your des-ti-ny,—
Will jus-ti-fy His ways at last, Leave it to Him,

CHORUS.

Him. . . Leave it to Him . . who knoweth all, . . .
leave it to Him. leave it to Him, leave it to Him,

Him who marks . . the sparrow's fall, . . Who lis-tens to the
Leave it to Him who marks the sparrow's fall,

ra-ven's call, Leave it to Him, leave it to Him. . . .
Leave it to Him, leave it to Him.

Copyright, 1891, by Chas. H. Gabriel.

No. 37. SAFE WITHIN THE VAIL.
J. M. EVANS.

1. "Land a-head!" its fruits are waving O'er the hills of fade-less green;
2. On-ward, bark! the cape I'm rounding; See the bless-ed wave their hands;
3. There, let go the an-chor, rid-ing On this calm and sil-v'ry bay;
4. Now we're safe from all temptation; All the storms of life are past;

And the liv-ing wa-ters lav-ing Shores where heav'nly forms are seen.
Hear the harps of God resound-ing, From the bright immor-tal bands.
Sea-ward fast the tide is glid-ing, Shores in sun-light glide a-way.
Praise the Rock of our sal-va-tion, We are safe at home at last.

CHORUS.
Rocks and storms I'll fear no more When on that e-ter-nal shore;
Drop the an-chor! Furl the sail! I am safe with-in the vail.

No. 38.

1 O happy day, that fixed my choice
 On Thee, my Saviour and my God!
Well may this glowing heart rejoice,
 And tell its raptures all abroad.

CHO.—Happy day, etc.

2 O happy bond, that seals my vows,
 To Him who merits all my love;
Let cheerful anthems fill His house,
 While to that sacred shrine I move.

3 'Tis done, the great transaction's done;
 I am my Lord's, and He is mine;
He drew me, and I followed on,
 Charmed to confess the voice divine.

TO THE CROSS. Concluded.

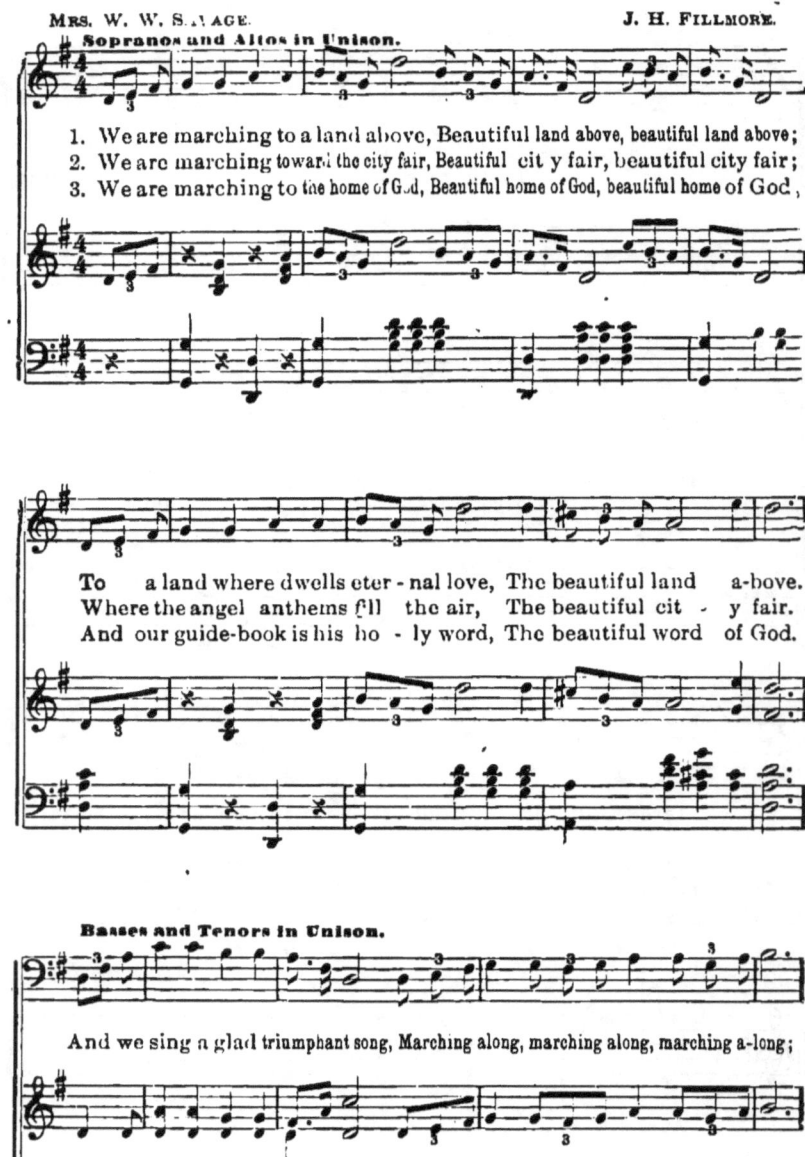

Marching to the Land Above. Concluded.

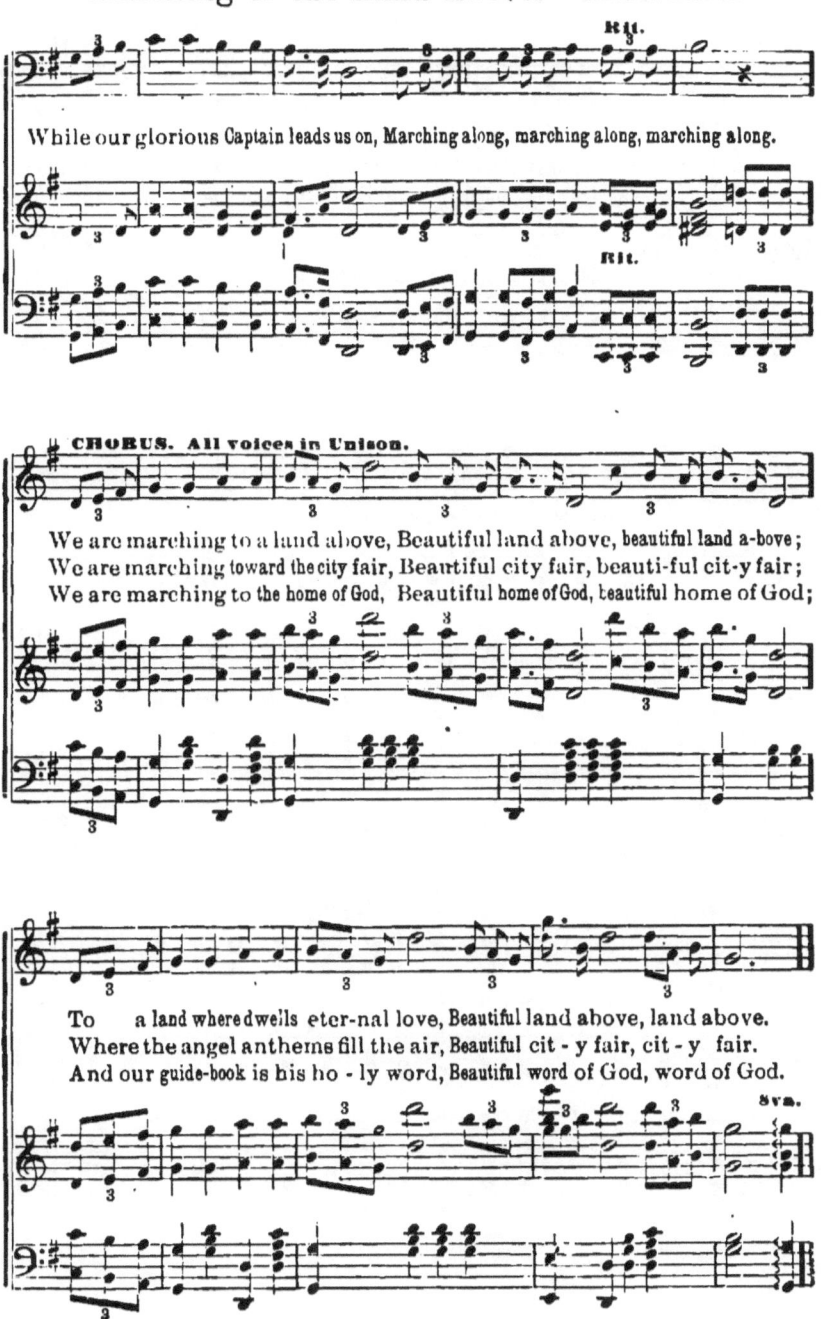

While our glorious Captain leads us on, Marching along, marching along, marching along.

CHORUS. All voices in Unison.

We are marching to a land above, Beautiful land above, beautiful land a-bove;
We are marching toward the city fair, Beautiful city fair, beauti-ful cit-y fair;
We are marching to the home of God, Beautiful home of God, beautiful home of God;

To a land where dwells eter-nal love, Beautiful land above, land above.
Where the angel anthems fill the air, Beautiful cit - y fair, cit - y fair.
And our guide-book is his ho - ly word, Beautiful word of God, word of God.

No. 42. MOVING TOWARD THE CITY.

"For here have we no continuing city, but seek for one to come"—HEB. 13: 14.

Mrs. E. W. CHAPMAN.   J. H. TENNEY.

1. We are mov-ing toward the Cit-y; Farther on we pitch our tents;
2. We are mov-ing toward the Cit-y; Resting not in fer - tile plains;
3. We are mov-ing toward the Cit-y; In the path the ransomed trod;

As we climb the greenclad high-lands, Glo-ry shines on us from thence.
Ev-'ry day's march brings us nearer Where the King of glo - ry reigns.
Tenting near-er, near-er, near - er To the pal-ace of our God.

CHORUS.

We are mov - ing with the Saviour for our guide;
We are moving with the Saviour for our guide, We are moving,

We are tent-ing near-er to fair Ca-naan's side.
for our guide; We are tent-ing near-er, near-er to Canaan's side, We are tenting near-er, near-er to

Copyright, 1895, by Charlie D. Tillman.

No. 43. ARE YOU WATCHING?

EMILY C. PEARSON. HAMP. H. SEWELL.

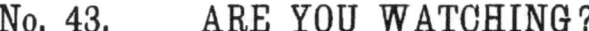

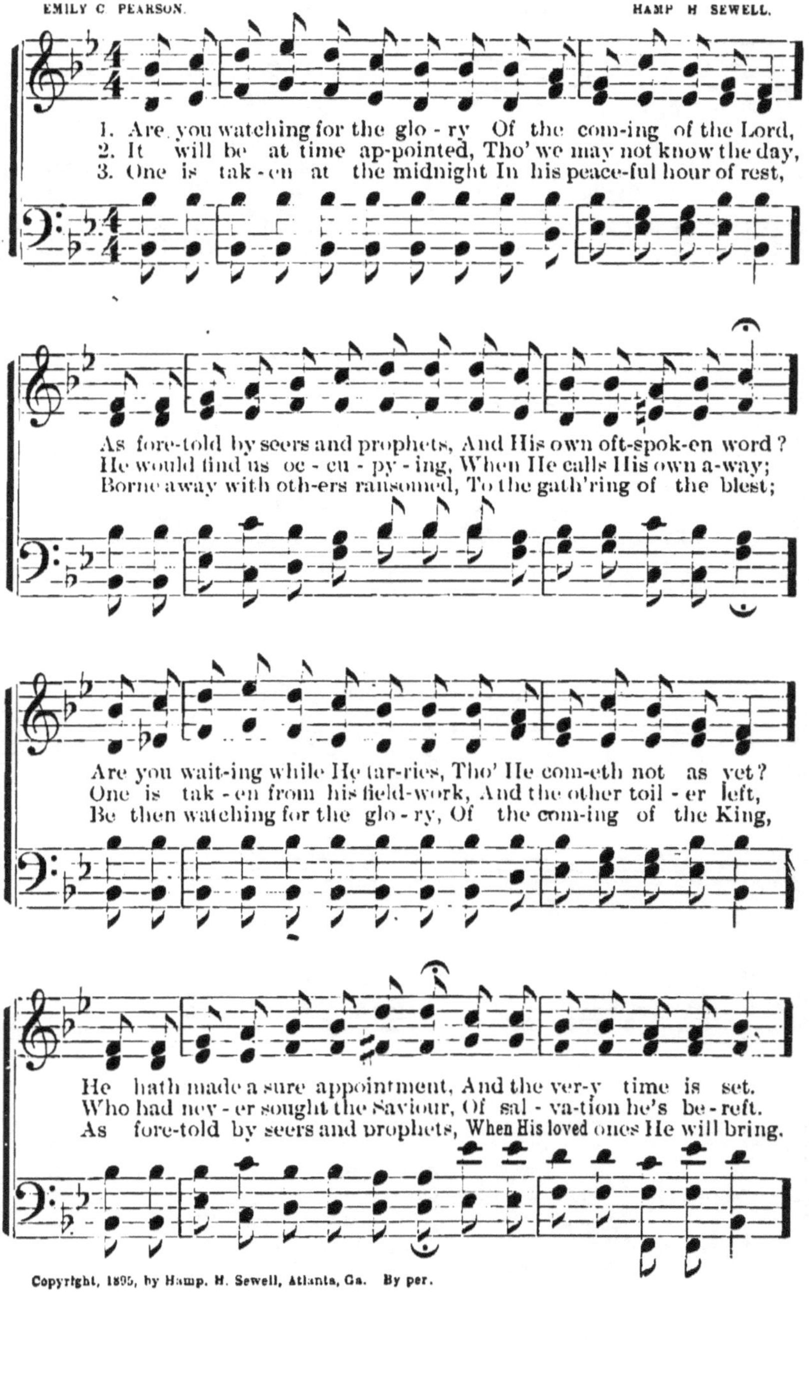

THE LAST CHANCE. Concluded.

WHITER THAN SNOW. Concluded.

No. 50. BLEST BE THE TIE.

JOHN FAWCETT.   GEO. NAEGEL

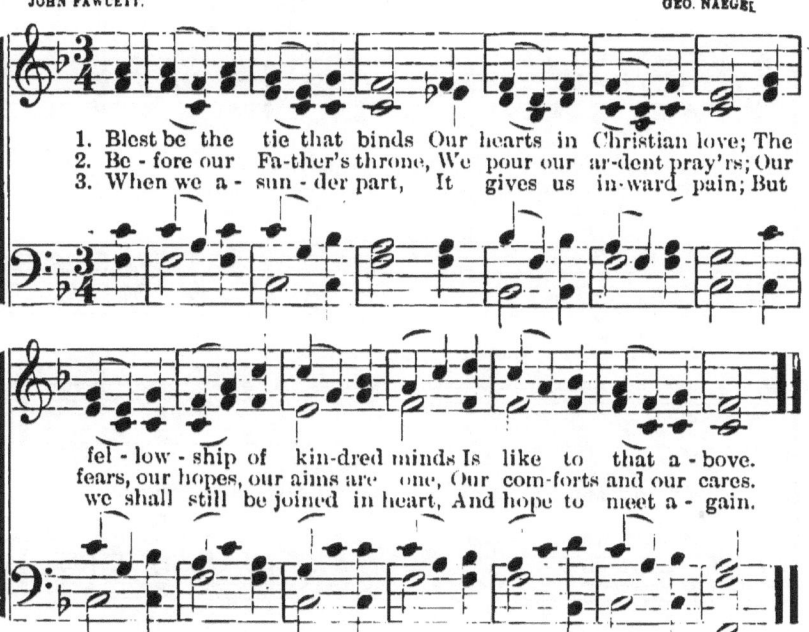

1. Blest be the tie that binds Our hearts in Christian love; The fel-low-ship of kin-dred minds Is like to that a-bove.
2. Be-fore our Fa-ther's throne, We pour our ar-dent pray'rs; Our fears, our hopes, our aims are one, Our com-forts and our cares.
3. When we a-sun-der part, It gives us in-ward pain; But we shall still be joined in heart, And hope to meet a-gain.

No. 53. On the Hills Beyond the River.

On the Hills Beyond the River.

ONCE FOR ALL. Concluded.

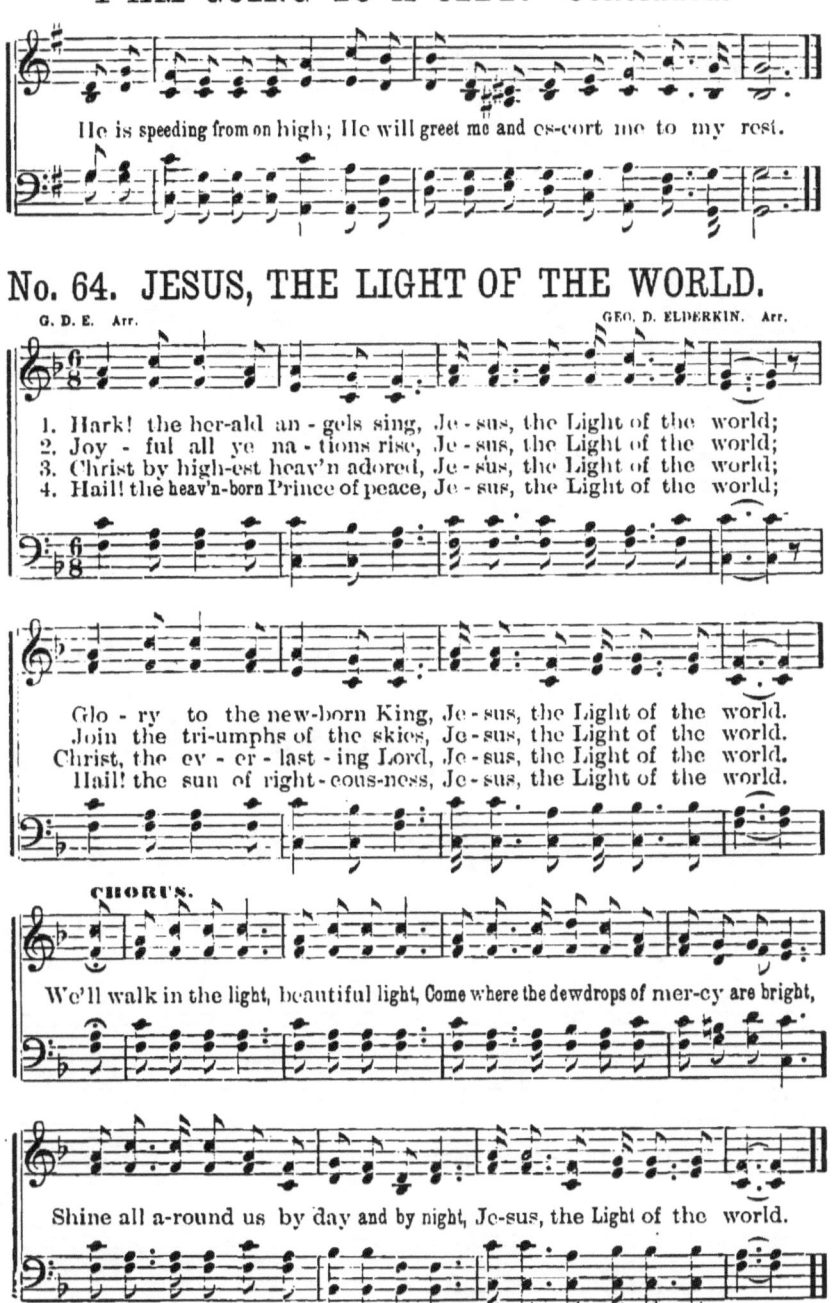

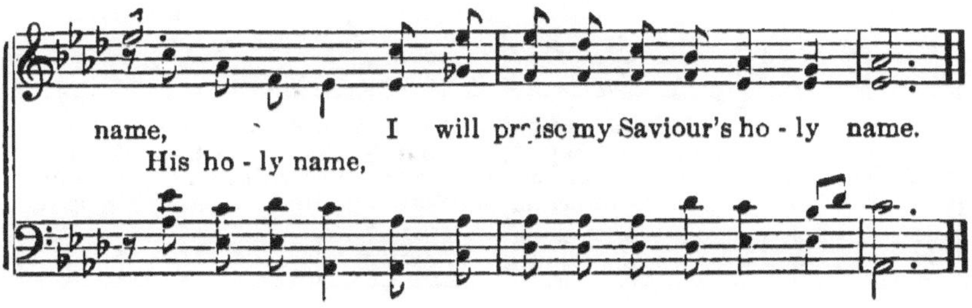

PRAISE HIS NAME. Concluded.

name, I will praise my Saviour's ho-ly name.
His ho-ly name,

No. 66. JESUS, SAVIOUR, PILOT ME.

Rev. Edward Hopper. D. D.   J. E. Gould.

1. Je-sus, Sav-iour, pi-lot me, O-ver Life's tempestuous sea,
2. As a moth-er stills her child, Thou canst hush the ocean wild;
3. When at last I near the shore, And the fear-ful breakers roar

Unknown waves around me roll, Hiding rock and treach'rous shoal,
Boist'rous waves obey Thy will, When Thou sayest "peace, be still;"
'Twixt me and my peaceful rest, Then while leaning on Thy breast,

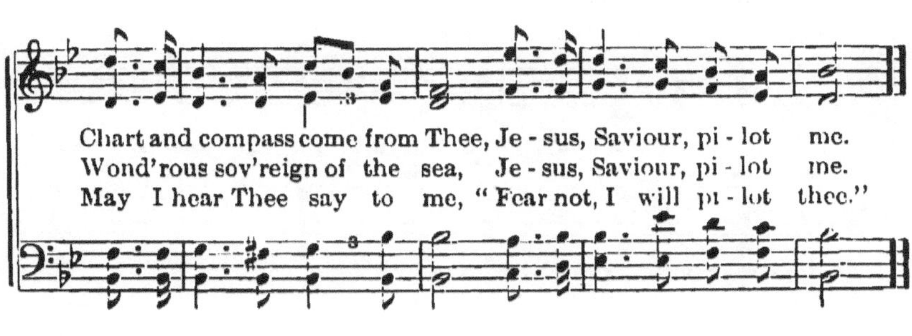

Chart and compass come from Thee, Je-sus, Saviour, pi-lot me.
Wond'rous sov'reign of the sea, Je-sus, Saviour, pi-lot me.
May I hear Thee say to me, "Fear not, I will pi-lot thee."

No. 67. THE DISPENSATION DAY.

B. E. W.   B. E. WARREN.

1. In the aw-ful age of night, When the earth was struck with blight, And the clouds of pa-pal darkness filled the sky; Per-se-cu-tion's fire and blood, Rag-ing in an an-gry flood, Failed to crush the Church, sustained by God on high.
2. But she raised her ban-ner high, And did all her foes de-fy, O-ver her the gates of hell have not pre-vailed; For her foes mul-ti-plied, Not-with-stand-ing those who died, In the martyr's flames her glo-ry was revealed.
3. Now the eve-ning time has come, When the brightness of the sun, Thro' the gos-pel shines in the re-mot-est land; It will reach the dis-tant isles, Where the gold-en harvest smiles, To be gathered while the Saviour's near at hand.
4. We are in the eve-ning light, Shin-ing in the morning light, And the clouds of thick ob-scur-i-ty are passed; In the conquest we are strong, Sing-ing as we march a-long, And we're read-y for the fi-nal trumpet's blast.

CHORUS.

We are in the evening of the dis-pen-sa-tion day, And the gos-pel light has scat-tered

Copyright, 1893, by Warner & Warren.

CHILDREN'S SONG. Concluded.

pours up-on us, When our lit-tle trib-ute to Him we bring.

Gestures to "CHILDREN'S SONG."

1. Extending hands.
2. Striking with both hands.
3. Left hand raised, right extended.
4. Right pointing to the right.
5 & 6. Two steps forward, placing even again.
7. Motioning right hand forward.
8. Right hand to heart.
9. Both hands raised beckoning.
10. Left forefinger to lips.
11. Showing both palms.
12. Motioning both hands to the left.
13. Covering eyes with left hand.
14. Peering forward.
15. Swaying body forward.
16. Casting both hands to left, downward.
17. Left hand clasping forehead.
18. Both hands raised, thrown out in opposite directions.
19. Both hands thrown out.
20. Kneeling down.
21. Left hand to lips.
22. Peering upward.
23. Left hand to ear, turning face a little to the right.
24. Folding arms.

No. 70. LITTLE SOLDIERS.

HAZEL MITCHELL, age 10 years.
H. M.   Har. by JOHN McPHERSON. By per.

1. Brave lit-tle sol-diers we must be, If the face of our Lord we see;
2. As I now walk with-in His path, He will keep me from sin and wrath;
3. Sure I am Je-sus' friend to-day, For He leads me a-long the way;
4. Marching along to heav'n's sweet land, Walking on at our Lord's com-mand,

Cho.—Oh, I love Je-sus, yes, I do, And I know that He loves me too;

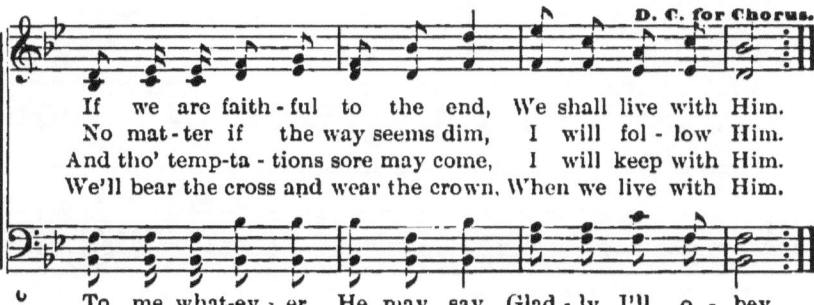

If we are faith-ful to the end, We shall live with Him.
No mat-ter if the way seems dim, I will fol-low Him.
And tho' temp-ta-tions sore may come, I will keep with Him.
We'll bear the cross and wear the crown, When we live with Him.

To me what-ev-er He may say, Glad-ly I'll o-bey.

SPEAK JUST A WORD. Concluded.

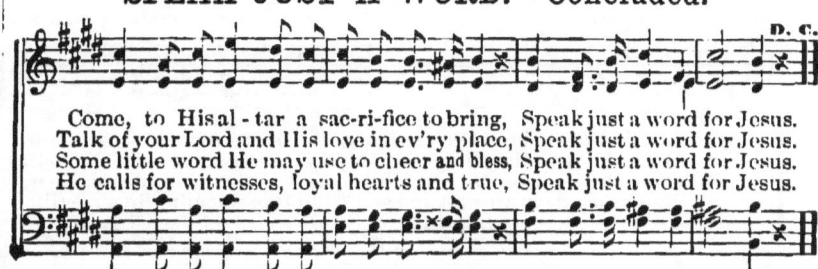

Come, to His altar a sacrifice to bring, Speak just a word for Jesus.
Talk of your Lord and His love in ev'ry place, Speak just a word for Jesus.
Some little word He may use to cheer and bless, Speak just a word for Jesus.
He calls for witnesses, loyal hearts and true, Speak just a word for Jesus.

No. 74.   THE GOSPEL FEAST.

CHARLEY WESLEY. "Come, for all things are ready."—LUKE 14: 16.   H. L. GILMOUR.
Cho. by H. L. G.

1. Come, sinners, to the gospel feast; It is for you, it is for me;
2. Ye need not one be left behind, It is for you, it is for me;

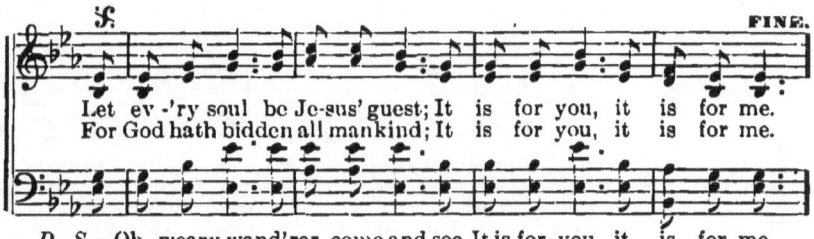

Let ev-'ry soul be Jesus' guest; It is for you, it is for me.
For God hath bidden all mankind; It is for you, it is for me.

D. S.—Oh, weary wand'rer, come and see, It is for you, it is for me.

CHORUS.

Salvation full, salvation free, The price was paid on Calvary;

3 Sent by my Lord, on you I call;
  The invitation is to all:
4 Come, all the world! come, sinner, thou!
  All things in Christ are ready now.
5 Come, all ye souls by sin oppressed,
  Ye restless wanderers after rest;
6 Ye poor, and maimed, and halt, and blind,
  In Christ a hearty welcome find.

7 My message as from God receive;
  Ye all may come to Christ and live:
8 Oh, let this love your hearts constrain,
  Nor suffer Him to die in vain.
9 See Him set forth before your eyes,
  That precious, bleeding sacrifice:
10 His offered benefits embrace,
   And freely now be saved by grace.

Copyright, 1889, by H. L. Gilmour.

MY MOTHER'S BIBLE. Concluded.

No. 76.   *Key of F.*

1 What a Friend we have in Jesus,
　All our sins and griefs to bear!
What a privilege to carry
　Every thing to God in prayer!
Oh, what peace we often forfeit,
　Oh, what needless pain we bear—
All because we do not carry
　Every thing to God in prayer.

2 Have we trials and temptations?
　Is there trouble anywhere?
We should never be discouraged,
　Take it to the Lord in prayer.
Can we find a friend so faithful,
　Who will all our sorrows share?
Jesus knows our every weakness;
　Take it to the Lord in prayer.

No. 77.   *Key of F.*

1 Work, for the night is coming,
　Work through the morning hours;
Work while the dew is sparkling,
　Work 'mid springing flowers;
Work when the day grows brighter,
　Work in the glowing sun;
Work, for the night is coming,
　When man's work is done.

2 Work, for the night is coming,
　Work through the sunny noon;
Fill brightest hours with labor,
　Rest comes sure and soon;
Give every flying minute
　Something to keep in store;
Work, for the night is coming,
　When man works no more.

THE LIFE-BOAT. Concluded.

4 Yes, see her coming o'er the tide
With banners all unfurled;
She comes from heavenly ports afar,
To take us from this world.
"Aboard, aboard," the Captain cries,
Let every pilgrim come,
And once upon the Life-boat,
I'll bear you safely home."

5 Behold all things are ready now,
The bells begin to ring,
The Captain stands upon the prow,
And all the pilgrims sing.
The breezes fill the canvas,
The waters rush and foam,
For we're upon the Life-boat,
And on our journey home.

6 Far out upon the widening seas
Our Captain steers the way,
And yonder in the eastern skies
We see the gleaming day.
Oh, yes, we see the distant shore,
We hear the ransomed sing,
And every breeze that comes this way
The sweetest odors bring.

7 Oh, wondrous joy we're home at last,
We've reached the golden shore!
And here we'll live, and sing, and praise,
And shout forever more.
We're welcomed by our Saviour here
And friends and loved ones come;
While angel throngs and ransomed saints
All bid us welcome home!

No. 79. SINNERS TURN; WHY WILL YE DIE?

REV. C. WESLEY, 1745.

1 Sinners, turn; why will ye die?
God, your Maker, asks you why?
God, who did your being give,
Made you with Himself to live;
He the fatal cause demands:
Asks the work of His own hands,—
Why, ye thankless creatures, why
Will ye cross His love, and die?

2 Sinners, turn; why will ye die?
God, your Saviour, asks you why?
He, who did your souls retrieve,
Died Himself, that ye might live.

Will ye let Him die in vain?
Crucify your Lord again?
Why, ye ransomed sinners, why
Will ye slight His grace and die?

3 Sinners, turn; why will ye die?
God, the Spirit, asks you why?
He who all your lives hath strove,
Urged you to embrace His love.
Will ye not His grace receive?
Will ye still refuse to live?
O ye dying sinners, why,
Why will ye forever die?

SOMETHING JESUS GAVE ME. Concluded.

To have,... to bear,... In meekness and in prayer.
To have, to bear,

No. 81. AT THE FOUNTAIN.

Old Melody.

1. Of Him who did sal-va-tion bring, I'm at the fountain drinking,
2. Ask but His grace and lo! 'tis giv'n, I'm at the fountain drinking,
3. Tho' sin and sor-row wound my soul, I'm at the fountain drinking,
4. Wher-e'er I am, where'er I move, I'm at the fountain drinking,
5. In - sa-tiate to this spring I fly, I'm at the fountain drinking

I could for - ev - er think and sing, I'm on my journey home.
Ask and He turns your hell to heav'n, I'm on my journey home.
Je - sus, Thy balm will make me whole, I'm on my journey home.
I meet the ob - ject of my love, I'm on my journey home.
I drink and yet am ev - er dry, I'm on my journey home.

CHORUS.

Glo - ry to God, I'm at the fountain drinking, on my journey home.

No. 85. ONE NARROW WAY.

JOHN 14:6; 10:9.

B. E. F.
Slow with expressione.

BIRDIE E. FINK

1. Only one narrow way, "I am *the* way," On-ly one o-pen door,
2. Only one mind and mouth, All speak the same, On-ly one church of God,
3. Oh, see His crimson blood, Flowing for all, Behold thy patient friend,

"I am *the* door." Only one Shepherd, kind, To heal the sick and blind,
Kept in His name. On-ly one gentle hand, To lead the lit-tle band;
Drinking life's gall. On-ly one rest complete, Low at His love-ly feet;

REFRAIN.

On-ly one reeking cross, For souls that are lost.
On-ly one ho-ly plain, One heaven to gain. On-ly one
On-ly one fountain free, 'Tis flowing for thee.

narrow way, "I am *the* way," On-ly one o-pen door, "I am *the* door."

Copyright, 1893, by Warner & Warren.

No. 86. AT THE CROSS.

R. E. HUDSON.

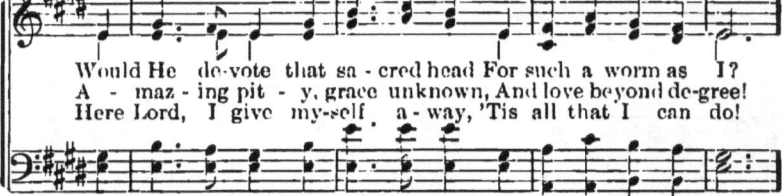

1. A-las! and did my Saviour bleed, And did my Sovereign die,
2. Was it for crimes that I have done, He groaned upon the tree?
3. But drops of grief can ne'er re-pay, The debt of love I owe;

Would He devote that sacred head For such a worm as I?
A-maz-ing pit-y, grace unknown, And love beyond degree!
Here Lord, I give my-self a-way, 'Tis all that I can do!

CHORUS.

At the cross, at the cross, where I first saw the light, And the burden of my heart rolled away— rolled a-way, It was there by faith

I received my sight, And now I am hap-py all the day.

Copyright, 1885, by R. E. Hudson. Used by per

No. 87. WE SHALL RUN AND NOT BE WEARY.

B. E. W.   Is. 40:31.   B. E. WARREN.

1. I now am running in the Christian race, To gain the promised prize;
2. We'll run and never fal-ter by the way, For Je-sus' word is true;
3. I'll stand upon His word and prove His pow'r, The Rock of A-ges past;
4. The heavy weights of sin are laid a-side, My heart is free and light;
5. When life is o'er and labor here is done, Can we thus say with Paul?—

Through Jesus' matchless, saving, keeping grace, We'll crown Him in the skies.
He's promised if we ev-er will o-bey, To bring us safe-ly through
I know He'll keep me, trusting ev'ry hour, While life on earth shall last.
There's nothing we may fear which can betide, Our hope is clear and bright.
"I've fought the fight and there's a starry crown," That's waiting for us all.

CHORUS.

We shall run . . . . . and not be wea-ry,
We shall run and not be wea-ry, we shall walk and never faint;

We shall walk . . . . and nev-er faint, . . . We're
We shall run and not be wea-ry, we shall walk and never faint;

trav'ling to our happy home, We'll walk and nev-er faint, (never faint.)

Copyright, 1893, by Warner and Warren.

No. 91. I KNOW MY NAME IS THERE.

"Rejoice because your names are written in heaven."—LUKE 10 : 20.

D. S. WARNER. B. E. WARREN. By per.

1. My name is in the Book of life, Oh, bless the name of Je - sus!
2. My name once stood with sinners, lost, And bore a painful rec-ord;
3. Yet inward trouble oft-en cast A shad-ow o'er my ti - tle;
4. While others climb thro' worldly strife, To carve a name of honor,

I rise a - bove all doubt and strife, And read my ti - tle clear.
But, by His blood the Saviour crossed, And placed it on His roll.
But, now with full sal-va - tion blest, Praise God! its ev-er clear.
High up in Heaven's Book of life, My name is writ-ten there.

CHORUS.

I know, I know my name is there;
I know, I tru - ly know, I know my name is there,
I know, I know my name is writ-ten there.
I know my name is there,

Second No. 90. Come to the Saviour.

Music on opposite page.

1 Jesus is calling, calling for thee,
Hearest thou not His importunate plea?
Oh, by the spear-wound pierced in His side,
Haste to be saved by the crucified.

FIRST, SECOND AND THIRD CHORUS.
Come to the Saviour, no longer delay,
Trust in His love and accept Him to-day ;
Tenderly, lovingly calls He to thee,
List to His pleading, believe and be free.

2 Jesus is pleading, pleading with thee,
Was ever mercy so rich and so free?
Wonderful grace He waits to bestow,
Is it not strange He should love thee so?

3 Jesus is waiting, waiting for thee,
Love could not purer and holier be,
Oh, for the blood poured out for thy soul,
Come to this Saviour and be made whole.

4 Jesus is here, but soon He may go,
Shall He bear with Him thy sins and thy woe?
Oh, then entreat Him, ere He depart,
Freely to pardon and cleanse thy heart.

LAST CHORUS.
Wonderful grace! how it satisfies me,
Wonderful mercy! so rich and so free;
Would you a child of the covenant be?
Jesus can save you—He sweetly saved me.

No. 92. THE MASTER CALLS FOR REAPERS.

M. W. KNAPP. L. L. PICKETT.

1. Hark! the Master calls for reapers; Rich and ripe the harvest, see.
   Idle not, but quickly flying, Answer, Lord, send me, send me.

CHORUS.
Spread the gospel invitation, Speak a warning, breathe a prayer;
All around you men are dying, You can find them ev'rywhere.

Copyrighted, 1894, by L. L Pickett.

2 Great the harvest, few the toilers,
   Work is waiting one and all;
   Answer quickly, and rejoicing,
   Hear and heed the Master's call.

3 Gather golden sheaves for Jesus,
   Ere too late, they ruined be;
   Great and precious is the harvest,
   And 't is Jesus calleth thee.

4 Rich reward is for thee waiting,
   If but faithful thou wilt prove;
   Christ will say, "Well done, thou faith-
   In His kingdom bright above. [ful,"

5 But if thou shouldst falsely linger,
   Proving thus to Him untrue,
   Fearful, then, will be the reckoning
   At the Judgment waiting you.

6 Jesus shed His blood so precious,
   On the cross for thee didst die;
   Therefore heed His call so earnest,
   Swiftly to the harvest fly.

No. 94. THE MUSIC OF HIS NAME.

D. S. WARNER.   "Sing for the honor of His name."—Ps. 66 : 2.   B. E. WARREN.

1. Who can sing the wondrous love of the Son Di-vine! Oh! my
2. Tune your hearts, ye ransomed throng, and extol the Christ: Sing the
3. Oh! let saints and an-gels join in tri-umph-ant song; Let the

Lord, there's none so dear to me, As the One who bore the
name that o-pened mer-cy's door, Oh! 'tis mu-sic, sweetest
mu-sic of all worlds ac-cord, And in ho-ly an-thems

bur-den of all my sin, And so free-ly died to set me free.
mu-sic to sin-ners lost, Sweetest to the saints for ev-er-more.
high o-ver all, pro-claim, Glo-ry be to Je-sus Christ the Lord.

CHORUS.

Oh, the pre-cious mu-sic of Je-sus' name!
Oh, the pre-cious, precious mu-sic of Je-sus' ho-ly name!

Glo-ry to the Lamb! . . Oh, sweetest name in song!
Glo-ry, glory to the precious Lamb, precious Lamb.

Copyright, 1893, by Warner and Warren.

THE MUSIC OF HIS NAME. Concluded.

All the heavens shall prolong The mu-sic of Thy name, (of Thy name.)

No. 95.   ENOUGH FOR ME.

Words and music by Rev. E. A. HOFFMAN, by per.

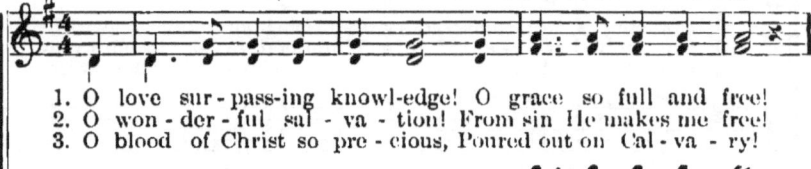

1. O love sur-pass-ing knowl-edge! O grace so full and free!
2. O won-der-ful sal-va-tion! From sin He makes me free!
3. O blood of Christ so pre-cious, Poured out on Cal-va-ry!

I know that Je-sus saves me, And that's e-nough for me!
I feel the sweet as-sur-ance, And that's e-nough for me!
I feel its cleans-ing pow-er, And that's e-nough for me!

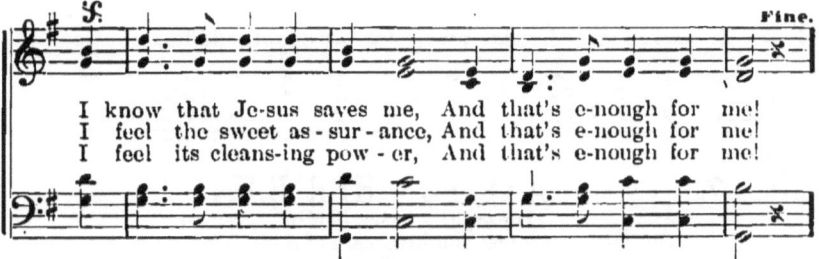

D. S. I know that Je-sus saves me, And that's e-nough for me!

REFRAIN.   D. S.

And that's e-nough for me! And that's e-nough for me!

4 Oh, wondrous love of Jesus,
  He tasted death for me;
He lives my King forever,
  And that's enough for me.

5 His blessed Holy Spirit
  With mine doth now agree;
He tells me—I'm adopted;
  And that's enough for me.

6 I have His sweet communion,
  He walks—and talks with me,
And fills my life with gladness—
  And that's enough for me.

7 His grace will be sufficient,
  Till I His glory see,
Then safe at home forever—
  And that's enough for me.

No. 96. CONVERT'S PRAISES.

E. S. U.
EDWARD S. UFFORD.

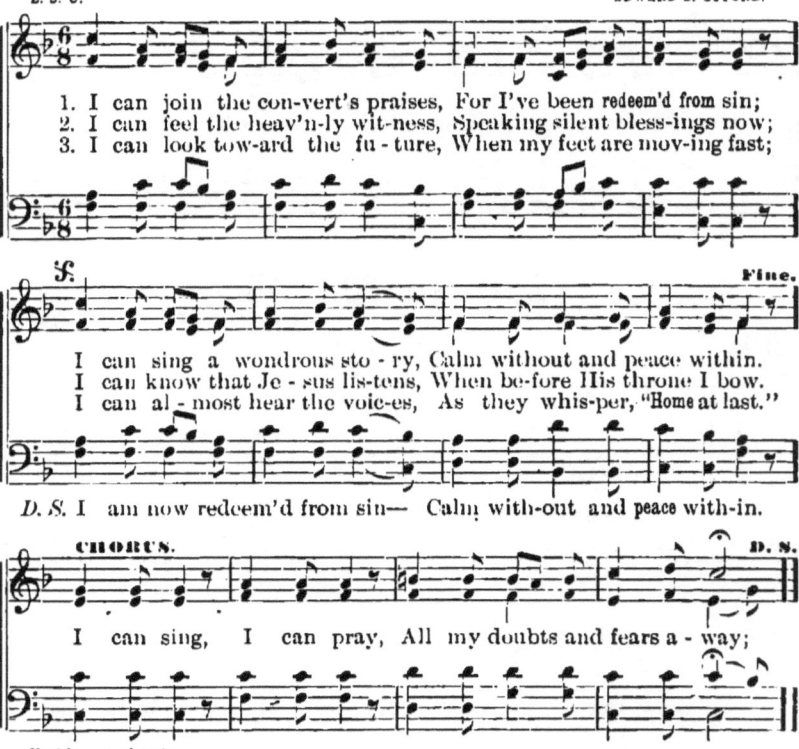

1. I can join the con-vert's praises, For I've been redeem'd from sin;
2. I can feel the heav'n-ly wit-ness, Speaking silent bless-ings now;
3. I can look tow-ard the fu-ture, When my feet are mov-ing fast;

I can sing a wondrous sto-ry, Calm without and peace within.
I can know that Je-sus lis-tens, When be-fore His throne I bow.
I can al-most hear the voic-es, As they whis-per, "Home at last."

D. S. I am now redeem'd from sin— Calm with-out and peace with-in.

CHORUS.

I can sing, I can pray, All my doubts and fears a-way;

Used by per. of Author.

No. 97. PRAYS FOR HER BOY.
TUNE—"Old Oaken Bucket."

1 Oh, who can forget the kind care of a mother?
  A mother who kneels down and prays for her boy,
  Who weeps at the altar and pleads as no other,
  For one gone astray who has blighted her joy.
  How anxious she watches when late home returning,
  To see if the tempter was leading astray;
  She's fearing and dreading, her loving heart yearning,
  Oh, what more can she do, but kneel there and pray?

REFRAIN.—Oh, she prays for her darling, with heart almost breaking;
  A mother who prays for her own precious boy.

2 How pale was her face, when her boy would come reeling,
  With his wild foolish talking, that chilled her dear heart,
  How little he thinks of her poor wounded feelings,
  Struggling to keep back the tears that do start.
  She even could wish the death-angel had taken,
  When safely to heaven he could have been borne;
  She sees her kind teachings, he now has forsaken,
  He thoughtlessly leaves her to pray and to mourn.

LAST REF.—Come now to mother's Saviour and He will receive you;
  If you come repentant He'll cleanse you from sin.

CHARLIE D. TILLMAN, from G. W. PAYNE.

No. 100. O FOR A THOUSAND TONGUES.

AZMON. C. M.

CHARLES WESLEY.   LOWELL MASON.

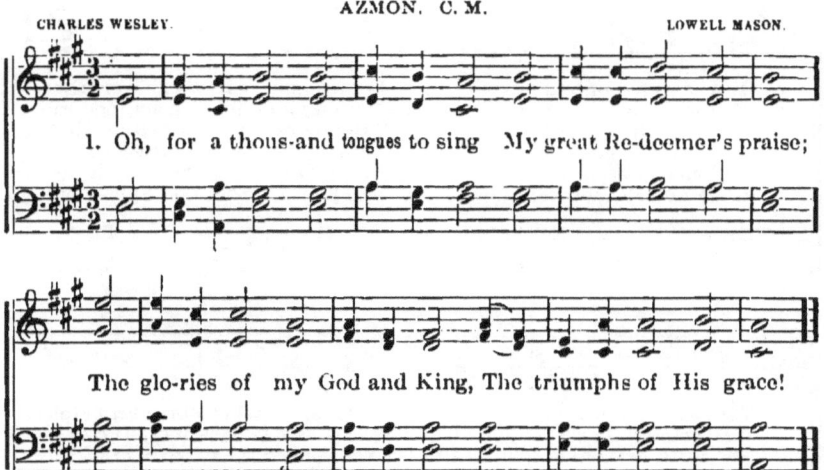

1. Oh, for a thous-and tongues to sing My great Re-deemer's praise;
The glo-ries of my God and King, The triumphs of His grace!

2 My gracious Master and my God,
  Assist me to proclaim,
To spread thro' all the earth abroad,
  The honors of Thy name.

3 Jesus! the name that charms our
  That bids our sorrows cease; [fears,
'Tis music in the sinner's ears,
  'Tis life, and health, and peace.

4 He breaks the power of canceled sin,
  He sets the prisoner free;
His blood can make the foulest clean,
  His blood availed for me.

No. 101.   *See music above.*

1 Salvation! Oh, the joyful sound,
  What pleasure to our ears?
A sovereign balm for every wound,
  A cordial for our fears.

2 Salvation! let the echo fly
  The spacious earth around,
While all the armies of the sky
  Conspire to raise the sound.

3 Salvation! O thou bleeding Lamb!
  To Thee all praise belongs:
Salvation shall inspire our hearts,
  And dwell upon our tongues.
                JOHN NEWTON.

No. 102.   *See music above.*

1 Oh, for a heart to praise my God,
  A heart from sin set free!
A heart that always feels Thy blood,
  So freely spilt for me!

2 A heart resigned, submissive, meek,
  My great Redeemer's throne;
Where only Christ is heard to speak,
  Where Jesus reigns alone.

3 Oh, for a lowly, contrite heart,
  Believing, true, and clean,
Which neither life nor death can part
  From Him that dwells within!

4 A heart in every thought renewed,
  And full of love divine, [good,
Perfect, and right, and pure, and
  A copy, Lord, of Thine.
                CHARLES WESLEY.

No. 103.   *See music above.*

1 Am I a soldier of The cross,
  A follower of the Lamb,
And shall I fear to own His cause,
  Or blush to speak His name?

2 Must I be carried to the skies
  On flowery beds of ease,
While others fought to win the prize,
  And sailed through bloody seas?

3 Are there no foes for me to face?
  Must I not stem the flood?
Is this vile world a friend to grace,
  To help me on to God?

4 Sure I must fight, if I would reign;
  Increase my courage, Lord;
I'll bear the toil, endure the pain;
  Supported by Thy word.
                ISAAC WATTS.

"Unto you, therefore, which believe He is precious."—1 PET. 2: 7.
To the memory of the late S. T. Gordon.   W. A. WILLIAMS.

1. I entered once a home of care, For age and pen-u-ry were there,
2. I stood beside a dy-ing bed, Where lay a child with aching head,
3. I saw the mar-tyr at the stake, The flames could not his courage shake,
4. I saw the gos-pel her-ald go,—To Af-ric's sand and Greenland's snow,
5. I dream'd that hoary Time had fled, And earth and sea gave up their dead,
6. Then come to Christ, oh! come to-day, The Fa-ther, Son, and Spir-it say,

Yet peace and joy withal; I asked the lonely mother whence Her helpless
Wait-ing for Je-sus' call; I mark'd his smile, 'twas sweet as May, And as his
Nor death his soul ap-pall, I ask'd him whence his strength was giv'n, He look'd tri-
To save from Satan's thrall; Nor home nor life he counted dear 'Midst wants and
A fire dis-solved this ball; I saw the church's ransom'd throng, I heard the
The Bride repeats the call; For He will cleanse your guilty stains, His love will

CHORUS.

wid-ow-hood's defense, She told me "Christ was all."
spir-it passed a-way, He whispered, "Christ is all."
umph-ant-ly to heav'n, And an-swered, "Christ is all." Christ is all, all in
per-ils owned no fear, He felt that "Christ is all."
bur-den of their song,'Twas "Christ is all in all."
soothe your weary pains, For "Christ is all in all."

all, yes, Christ is all in all,
all, (Omit) . . . . Yes, Christ is all in all.

Copyright, 1884, by S. T. Gordon & Son, by per.

No. 105. STAND UP, STAND UP FOR JESUS.

GEO. DUFFIELD.   WEBB. 7s. 6s.   GEO. WEBB.

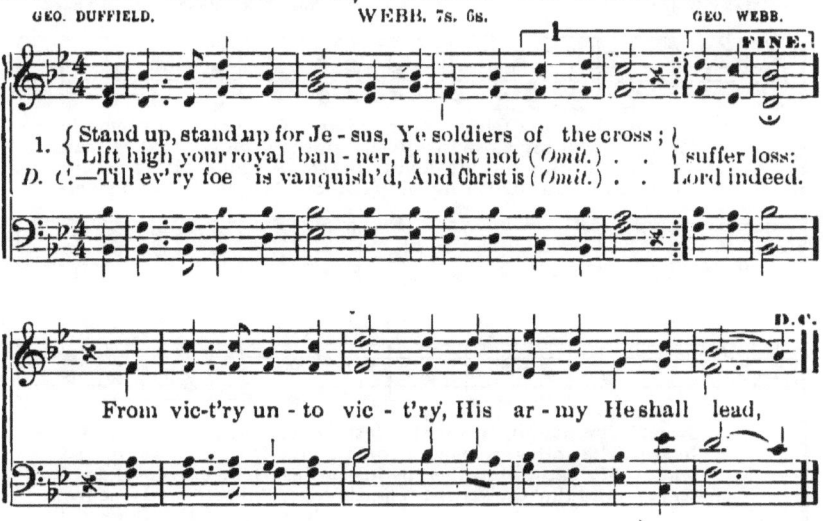

1. Stand up, stand up for Je-sus, Ye soldiers of the cross;
Lift high your royal ban-ner, It must not (*Omit.*) . . suffer loss:
D. C.—Till ev'ry foe is vanquish'd, And Christ is (*Omit.*) . . Lord indeed.

From vic-t'ry un-to vic-t'ry, His ar-my He shall lead,

2 Stand up, stand up for Jesus,
The trumpet call obey ;
Forth to the mighty conflict,
In this His glorious day:
"Ye that are men, now serve Him,"
Against unnumbered foes ;
Your courage rise with danger
And strength to strength oppose.

3 Stand up, stand up for Jesus,
Stand in His strength alone ;
The arm of flesh will fail you,
Ye dare not trust your own ;
Put on the gospel armor,
Each piece put on with prayer,
Where duty calls, or danger,
Be never wanting there.

No. 106. (*See music above.*)

1 The morning light is breaking ;
The darkness disappears ;
The sons of earth are waking,
To penitential tears:
Each breeze that sweeps the ocean,
Brings tidings from afar ;
Of nations in commotion,
Prepared for Zion's war.

2 See heathen nations bending,
Before the God of love,
And thousand hearts ascending,
In gratitude above ;
While sinners, now confessing,
The gospel's call obey,
And seek a Saviour's blessing,
A nation in a day.

3 Blest river of salvation,
Pursue thy onward way ;
Flow thou to every nation
Nor in thy richness stay:
Stay not till all the lowly,
Triumphant reach their home ;
Stay not till all the holy
Proclaim "The Lord is come!"

No. 107. (*See music above.*)

1 Unfurl the Temp'rance Banner,
And fling it to the breeze,
And let the glad hosanna
Sweep over land and seas ;
To God be all the glory
For what we now behold—
Oh, let the cheering story
In every ear be told.

2 The drunkard shall not perish
In Alcohol's dire chain,
But wife and children cherish
Within his home again ;
And sobered men, repenting,
Will bow at Jesus' feet,
Their thankful hearts relenting
Before the mercy-seat.

3 A new-waked zeal is burning
In this and every land,
And thousands now are turning
To join our temp'rance band ;
The light of truth is shining
In many a darkened soul ;
Ere long its rays combining
Will blaze from pole to pole.

No. 108. COMPANIONSHIP WITH JESUS.

MARY D. JAMES. WM. J. KIRKPATRICK. By per.

1. Oh, bless-ed fellow-ship divine! Oh, joy supreme-ly sweet! Companionship with Jesus here Makes life with bliss re-plete: In un-ion with the purest one, I find my heav'n on earth be-gun.
2. I'm walking close to Jesus' side; So close that I can hear The softest whispers of his love In fel-lowship so dear, And feel his great Almighty hand Protects me in this hos-tile land.
3. I'm leaning on his loving breast, A-long life's weary way; My path, illumined by his smiles, Grows brighter day by day: No foes, no woes my heart can fear, With my Almigh-ty Friend so near.
4. I know his shelt'ring wings of love Are al-ways o'er me spread; And tho' the storms may fiercely rage, All calm and free from dread, My peaceful spir-it ev-er sings, "I'll trust the cov-ert of thy wings."

REFRAIN.

Oh, wondrous bliss! oh, joy sublime! I've

COMPANIONSHIP WITH JESUS. Concluded.

Je - sus with me all the time! Oh, wondrous bliss! oh, joy sub - lime! I've Je - sus with me all the time!

No. 109. THE COMING DAY.

1. And must I be to judgment brought, And answer in that day
For ev-'ry vain and i - dle thought, And ev-ry word I say?

CHORUS.

Oh, what will you do in the coming day, In the coming day, the coming day? When the heav'ns and the earth shall pass a - way, What will you do in that day?

2 Yes, every secret of my heart
   Shall shortly be made known,
And I receive my just desert
   For all that I have done.—Cho.

3 How careful then ought I to live,
   With that religious fear;
Who such a strict account must give
   For my behavior here.—Cho.

4 Thou awful Judge of quick and dead,
   The watchful power bestow;
So shall I to my ways take heed,—
   To all I speak or do.—Cho.

5 If now Thou standest at the door,
   Oh, let me feel Thee near;
And make my peace with God, before
   I at Thy bar appear.—Cho.

No. 110. *Music No. 143.*

1 See Jesus Thy disciples see.
   The promised blessing give,
Within Thy name we look to Thee,
   Expecting to receive.

2 Thee we expect our faithful Lord
   Who in Thy name are joined;
We wait according to Thy Word,
   Thee in the midst to find.

3 With us Thou art assembled here,
   But, oh, Thyself reveal!
Son of the living God appear
   Let us Thy presence feel.

4 Breathe on us Lord, in this our day,
   And these dry bones shall live,
Speak peace into our hearts and say
   The Holy Ghost receive.

No. 111. WITNESS FOR CHRIST.

"Tell how great things the Lord hath done for thee."—MARK 5: 9.

TABOR.   G. TABOR THOMPSON.

1. Are you walk-ing with the Lord? Tell it out! Tell it out!
2. Does your heart beat hot with-in? Tell it out! Tell it out!
3. Do you love this sa-cred hour? Tell it out! Tell it out!
5. Is your hope of glo-ry bright? Tell it out! Tell it out!

Speak for Him a lov-ing word, Tell it out! Tell it out!
Are you saved from in-bred sin? Tell it out! Tell it out!
Have you sanc-ti-fy-ing pow'r? Tell it out! Tell it out!
Are you liv-ing in the light? Tell it out! Tell it out!

He will all your be-ing fill, While you do His ho-ly will,
Does the blessing o-ver-flow? Then let all the peo-ple know;
Are you ev-'ry whit made whole? Does He wit-ness with your soul?
Christ will then confess for you, In that land be-yond the blue!

Tho' you're tempted to keep still, Tell it out! Tell it out!
Wit-ness-es for Christ be-low, Tell it out! Tell it out!
Let the tes-ti-mo-ny roll, Tell it out! Tell it out!
'Tis your turn, what will you do? Tell it out! Tell it out!

CHORUS.

Tell it out! Tell it out! Tell it
      Tell it out!   Tell it out!

Copyright, 1894, by G. Tabor Thompson.

No. 113. THE LOYAL ARMY.

"Out of weakness were made strong, waxed valiant in fight."—HEB. 11:34.

W. C. BROWN, Arr. by W. A. O. A. B. KAUFFMAN, Arr. by W. A. O.

1. We've en-list-ed in the ar-my, in the ar-my of the Lord,
2. In this grand and glorious ar-my there is room for ev-'ry one
3. Let us march a-long to-geth-er, comrades, fearlessly and bold,

We will la-bor in His ser-vice and o-bey His ho-ly word;
Who will wear the gos-pel ar-mor and go marching bravely on;
Loy-al sol-diers of the le-gion like the pa-tri-archs of old;

We will ga-ther up the fragments here that nothing may be lost,
If you can-not preach the gospel, you a word for Christ can say
Let us swell the joy-ful chorus in a song of loud ac-claim,

For the precious blood of Je-sus paid the fear-ful cost.
To en-cour-age lit-tle sol-diers now up-on the way.
Hal-le-lu-jah, hal-le-lu-jah to the Sav-iour's name.

CHORUS

March-ing on . . . so glad and free, . . . March-ing
Marching on so glad and free,

By permission.

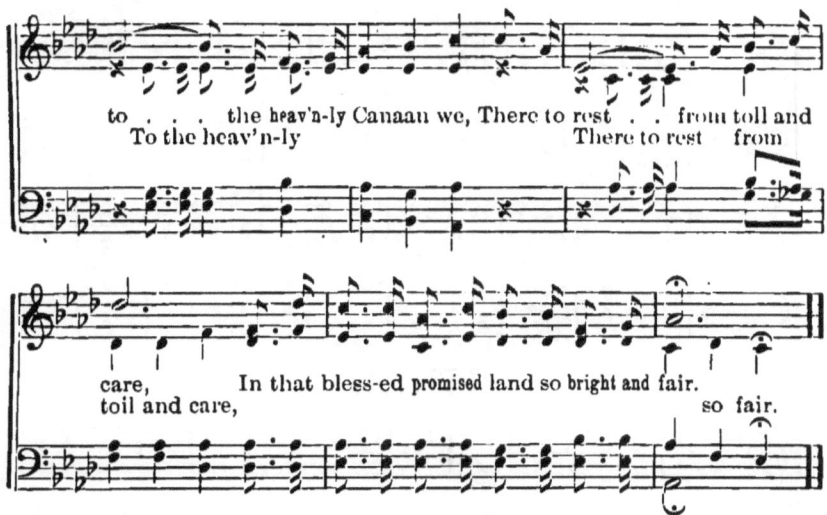

No. 115. Gracious Spirit, Love Divine.
See music above.

1 Gracious Spirit, love divine,
Let Thy light within me shine!
All my guilty fears remove;
Fill me with Thy heavenly love.

2 Speak Thy pardoning grace to me;
Set the burdened sinner free;
Lead me to the Lamb of God;
Wash me in His precious blood.

3 Life and peace to me impart;
Seal salvation on my heart;
Breathe Thyself into my breast,
Earnest of immortal rest.

4 Let me never from Thee stray;
Keep me in the narrow way;
Fill my soul with joy divine;
Keep me, Lord, forever Thine.
J. STOCKER.

No. 116. Holy Ghost, with Light Divine.
See music above.

1 Holy Ghost, with light divine,
Shine upon this heart of mine;
Chase the shades of night away,
Turn my darkness into day.

2 Holy Ghost, with power divine.
Cleanse this guilty heart of mine;
Long hath sin, without control,
Held dominion o'er my soul.

3 Holy Ghost, with joy divine,
Cheer this saddened heart of mine;
Bid my many woes depart,
Heal my wounded, bleeding heart.

4 Holy Spirit, all divine,
Dwell within this heart of mine;
Cast down every idol-throne,
Reign supreme—and reign alone.

No. 120. *Music No. 117.*

1 Joy to the world! the Lord is come;
  Let earth receive her King;
  Let every heart prepare Him room,
  And heaven and nature sing.

2 Joy to the world! the Saviour reigns;
  Let men their songs employ;
  While fields and floods, rocks, hills and
  Repeat the sounding joy.   [plains,

3 No more let sin and sorrow grow,
  Nor thorns infest the ground;
  He comes to make His blessings flow
  Far as the curse is found.

4 He rules the world with truth and grace
  And makes the nations prove
  The glories of His righteousness,
  And wonders of His love.

No. 121. *Music No. 118.*

1 Arise, my soul, arise;
  Shake off thy guilty fears;
  The bleeding sacrifice
  In my behalf appears;
  Before the throne my surety stands,
  My name is written on His hands.

2 He ever lives above
  For me to intercede,
  His all-redeeming love,
  His precious blood to plead;
  His blood atoned for all our race,
  And sprinkles now the throne of
  grace.

3 The Father hears Him pray,
  His dear annointed one;
  He can not turn away
  The presence of His Son;
  His Spirit answers to the blood,
  And tells me I am born of God.

4 My God is reconciled;
  His pard'ning voice I hear;
  He owns me for his child;
  I can no longer fear;
  With confidence I now draw nigh,
  And Father, Abba, Father, cry.

No. 122. *Music No. 118.*

1 Blow ye the trumpet, blow,
  The gladly solemn sound;
  Let all the nations know,
  To earth's remotest bound,
  The year of jubilee is come;
  Return, ye ransomed sinners, home.

2 Jesus, our great High Priest,
  Hath full atonement made;
  Ye weary spirits, rest;
  Ye mournful souls, be glad;
  The year of jubilee is come;
  Return, ye ransomed sinners, home.

3 Extol the Lamb of God,—
  The all-atoning Lamb;
  Redemption in His blood
  Throughout the world proclaim;
  The year of jubilee is come;
  Return, ye ransomed sinners, home.

No. 123. *Music No. 119.*

1 While life prolongs its precious light,
  Mercy is found and peace is given;
  But soon, ah, soon, approaching night
  Shall blot out every hope of heaven.

2 While God invites, how blest the day!
  How sweet the Gospel's charming
  sound!
  Come, sinners, haste, O haste away,
  While yet a pardoning God is found.

3 Soon, borne on times' most rapid wing,
  Shall death demand you to the grave,
  Before His bar your spirit bring,
  And none be found to hear or save.

4 In that lone land of deep despair,
  No Sabbath's heavenly light shall
  rise,
  No God regard your bitter prayer,
  No Saviour call you to the skies.

No. 124. BEYOND THE GRAVE.

(Can be sung to tune, 'Flowers from
Angel Mother's Grave.')

1 In the days long gone by when your
  childish play was done,
  And you knelt down beside mother's chair,
  Little did you think that in days that
  soon would come
  You would leave mother's God and
  mother's prayer.
  But you left your home, and mother's
  heart was broken when you fell,
  When she saw the demons chain
  you; as a slave
  And the lips that kissed her darling
  when the evening prayers were
  said;
  For long years have been mouldering
  in the grave.

  CHORUS.
  Onward you are drifting, drifting day
  by day,
  Soon, you will sink beneath the wave,
  Will you meet those gone before,
  On that happy golden shore,
  Or be banished from their home, be-
  yond the grave?

2 As they knelt by her side there to hear
  the last good-bye
  From the lips that once kissed away
  your care,
  Came the last whispering words as she
  pointed toward the sky:
  "Tell my loved ones to meet me over
  there."
  Death's cold waters rose around her as
  the life stream ebbed away,
  Then the Boatman came and took
  her 'cross the wave;
  Though the mists now hide her from
  you, still she's waiting over there.
  Will you meet her again beyond the
  grave.

No. 128. *Music No. 125.*

1 My faith looks up to Thee,
   Thou Lamb of Calvary,
      Saviour divine;
   Now hear me while I pray,
   Take all my guilt away,
   O let me from this day
      Be wholly thine.

2 May thy rich grace impart
   Strength to my fainting heart,
      My zeal inspire;
   As Thou hast died for me,
   O may my love to Thee
   Pure, warm, and changeless be—
      A living fire.

3 While life's dark maze I tread,
   And griefs around me spread,
      Be Thou my guide;
   Bid darkness turn to day,
   Wipe sorrow's tear away,
   Nor let me ever stray
      From thee aside.

No. 129. *Music No. 125.*

1 My country ! 'tis of thee,
   Sweet land of liberty,
      Of thee I sing ;
   Land where my fathers died !
   Land of the pilgrim's pride!
   From every mountain side
      Let freedom ring !

2 My native country thee,
   Land of the noble, free,
      Thy name I love;
   I love thy rocks and rills,
   Thy woods and templed hills:
   My heart with rapture thrills
      Like that above.

3 Our father's God! to Thee,
   Author of liberty,
      To Thee we sing ;
   Long may our land be bright
   With freedom's holy light;
   Protect us by Thy might,
      Great God, our King!

No. 130. *Music No. 127.*

1 Holy Spirit, faithful Guide,
   Ever near the Christian's side,
   Gently lead us by the hand,
   Pilgrims in a desert land.
   Weary souls fore'er rejoice,
   While they hear that sweetest voice,
   Whisp'ring softly, wanderer, come !
   Follow me, I'll guide thee home.

2 Ever present, truest friend,
   Ever near, thine aid to lend,
   Leave us not to doubt and fear,
   Groping on in darkness drear.
   When the storms are raging sore,
   Hearts grow faint and hopes give o'er
   Whisper softly, wanderer, come!
   Follow me, I'll guide thee home.

No. 131. *Music No. 126.*

1 How sweet the name of Jesus sounds
      In a believer's ear!
   It soothes his sorrow, heals his wounds
      And drives away his fear.

2 It makes the wounded spirit whole,
      And calms the troubled breast ;
   'Tis manna to the hungry soul,
      And to the weary rest.

3 Till then I would thy love proclaim
      With every fleeting breath ;
   And may the music of Thy name
      Refresh my soul in death.

No. 132. *Music No. 126.*

1 Oh for a faith that will not shrink,
      Though pressed by every foe,
   That will not tremble on the brink
      Of any earthly woe;—

2 A faith that shines more bright and clear
      When tempests rage without ;
   That when in danger knows no fear,
      In darkness feels no doubt ;—

3 A faith that keeps the narrow way
      Till lifes last hour is fled,
   And with a pure and heavenly ray
      Illumes a dying bed.

No. 133. *Music No. 126.*

1 O for a closer walk with God,
      A calm and heavenly frame;
   A light to shine upon the road
      That leads me to the Lamb !

2 Where is the blessedness I knew,
      When first I saw the Lord?
   Where is the soul-refreshing view
      Of Jesus and His word ?

3 Return, O holy dove, return,
      Sweet messenger of rest !
   I hate the sins that made Thee mourn
      And drove Thee from my breast.

4 The dearest idol I have known,
      Whate'er that idol be,
   Help me to tear it from my throne,
      And worship only Thee.

No. 137.   *Music No. 134.*

1 Hark, the voice of Jesus crying,
   "Who will go and work to-day?
  Fields are white and harvest waiting,
   Who will bear the sheaves away?"
  Loud and strong the Master calleth;
   Rich reward He offers thee;
  Who will answer gladly saying,
   "Here am I; send me, send me."

2 Let none hear you idly saying,
   "There is nothing I can do,"
  While the souls of men are dying,
   And the Master calls for you.
  Take the task He gives you gladly;
   Let His work your pleasure be;
  Answer quickly when He calleth,
   "Here am I, send, me, send me!"

No. 138.   *Music No. 135.*

1 Rock of Ages cleft for me,
  Let me hide myself in Thee
  Let the water and the blood,
  From Thy wounded side which flow'd
  Be of sin the double cure;
  Save from wrath, and make me pure.

2 Could my tears forever flow—
  Could my zeal no languor know—
  These for sin could not atone;
  Thou must save and Thou alone;
  In my hand no price I bring;
  Simply to Thy cross I cling.

3 While I draw this fleeting breath,
  When my eyes shall close in death,
  When I rise to worlds unknown,
  And behold Thee on Thy throne—
  Rock of Ages, cleft for me,
  Let me hide myself in Thee.

No. 139.   Down at the Saviour's Feet.
Tune—Down by the Old Mill Stream.

1 I'm glad I ever heard the blessed story
   Of love so full and free,
  That gave up all of Heaven and its glory,
   And bore all the sufferings for me;
  I'm glad that ere with broken heart
   I sought the mercy seat,
  And found relief from my load of sin and grief,
   While kneeling at the Saviour's feet.
  Praise the Lord,

CHORUS.
  Down at the Saviour's feet,
   Love finds its heaven all complete;
  Burdens roll away—
   Darkness turns to day,
  While kneeling at the Saviour's feet.

2 The world with all its joys no longer charms me,
   For purer bliss is mine;
  The tempter with his darts no longer harms me,
   While kept by the power that's divine,
  From inward strife and fear set free;
   My victory is complete,
  In joy or pain, in earthly loss or gain,
   I have heaven at the Saviour's feet.
  Praise the Lord, etc.

No. 140.   *Music No. 136.*

1 Just as I am without one plea,
  But that Thy blood was shed for me.
  And that Thou bidst me come to Thee
   O, Lamb of God, I come, I come!

2 Just as I am, and waiting not
  To rid my soul of one dark blot, [spot.
  To Thee whose blood can cleanse each
   O, Lamb of God, I come, I come!

3 Just as I am, thou wilt receive,
  Wilt welcome, pardon, cleanse, relieve,
  Because Thy promise I believe,
   O, Lamb of God, I come, I come!

4 Just as I am, Thy love unknown,
  Has broken every barrier down;
  Now to be Thine, yea, Thine alone,
   O Lamb of God, I come, I come!

No. 141.   *Music No. 136.*

1 Lord, I am Thine, entirely Thine,
  Purchased and saved by blood divine
  With full consent Thine I would be
  And own Thy sovereign right in me.

2 Grant one poor sinner more a place
  Among the children of Thy grace;
  A wretched sinner, lost to God,
  But ransomed by Immanuel's blood.

3 Thine would I live, Thine would I die
  Be Thine through all eternity;
  The vow is past beyond repeal,
  And now I set the solemn seal.

4 Here, at the cross where flows the blood
  That bought my guilty soul for God,
  Thee, my new Master, now I call,
  And consecrate to Thee my all,

No. 142.   *Music No. 134.*

1 Love divine all love excelling,
  Joy of heaven to earth come down;
  Fix in us Thy humble dwelling,
  All Thy faithful mercies crown;
  Jesus Thou art all compassion,—
  Pure, unbounded love Thou art;
  Visit us with Thy salvation,
  Enter every trembling heart.

2 Come, almighty to deliver,
  Let us all Thy life receive;
  Suddenly return, and never,
  Never more Thy temples leave;
  Thee we would be always blessing,
  Serve Thee as Thy hosts above,
  Pray and praise Thee without ceasing
  Glory in Thy perfect love.

No. 143. Must Jesus Bear the Cross Alone?

MAITLAND. C. M.

THOS. SHEPHERD. GEO. N. ALLEN.

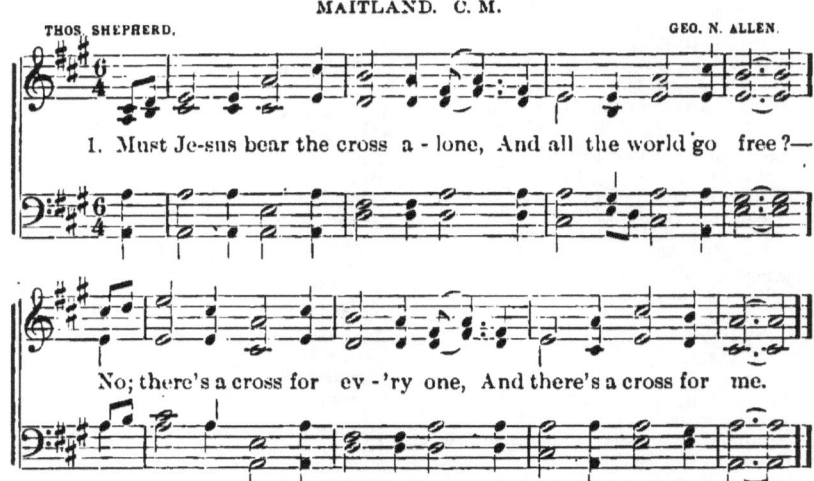

1. Must Jesus bear the cross alone, And all the world go free?—
No; there's a cross for ev-'ry one, And there's a cross for me.

2 The consecrated cross I'll bear,
  Till death shall set me free,
And then go home my crown to wear,
  For there's a crown for me.

3 Upon the crystal pavement, down,
  At Jesus' piercèd feet,
Joyful, I'll cast my golden crown,
  And His dear name repeat.

4 O precious cross! O glorious crown!
  O resurrection day!
Ye angels from the stars come down,
  And bear my soul away.

No. 144. *See music above.*

1 Come, Holy Spirit, Heavenly Dove,
  With all Thy quickening powers;
Kindle a flame of sacred love
  In these cold hearts of ours.

2 Look how we grovel here below,
  Fond of these earthly toys;
Our souls how heavily they go,
  To reach eternal joys.

3 In vain we tune our formal songs
  In vain we strive to rise;
Hosannas languish on our tongues,
  And our devotion dies.

No. 145. *See music above.*

1 Jesus commands us to forgive
  If we would be forgiven;
And Christians be while here on earth
  Or reign with Him in heaven.

Cho.—I must forgive, I do forgive
  My every enemy;
For Jesus shed His precious blood
  That He might pardon me.

2 Tho' deeply wronged we may have been,
  Our wrongs do not exceed
The insults we have heaped on Him
  Who for our sins did bleed.

3 He for His foes did suffer death,
  And freely all forgave;
And perished on the cruel cross
  That He their souls might save.

4 For those who pierced His hands and feet,
  Our Saviour prayed "Forgive;"
His Spirit we must all possess
  If we with Him would live.

5 O God, Thy Spirit now impart,
  That I Thine own may be;
That all my foes I may forgive
  As Thou forgivest me.

M. W. KNAPP. Used by per.

No. 146. *See music above.*

1 Amazing grace, how sweet the sound,
  That saved a wretch like me;
I once was lost, but now am found
  Was blind but now I see.

2 Thro' many dangers, toils and snares,
  I have already come;
'Tis grace has bro't me safe thus far,
  And grace will lead me home.

3 The Lord hath promised good to me,
  His word my hope secures;
He will my shield and portion be
  As long as life endures.

No. 147. I'M BELIEVING AND RECEIVING.

"Believing, ye rejoice with joy unspeakable." 1 Pet. 1:8.

H. H. R.   Commandant HERBERT BOOTH, by per.

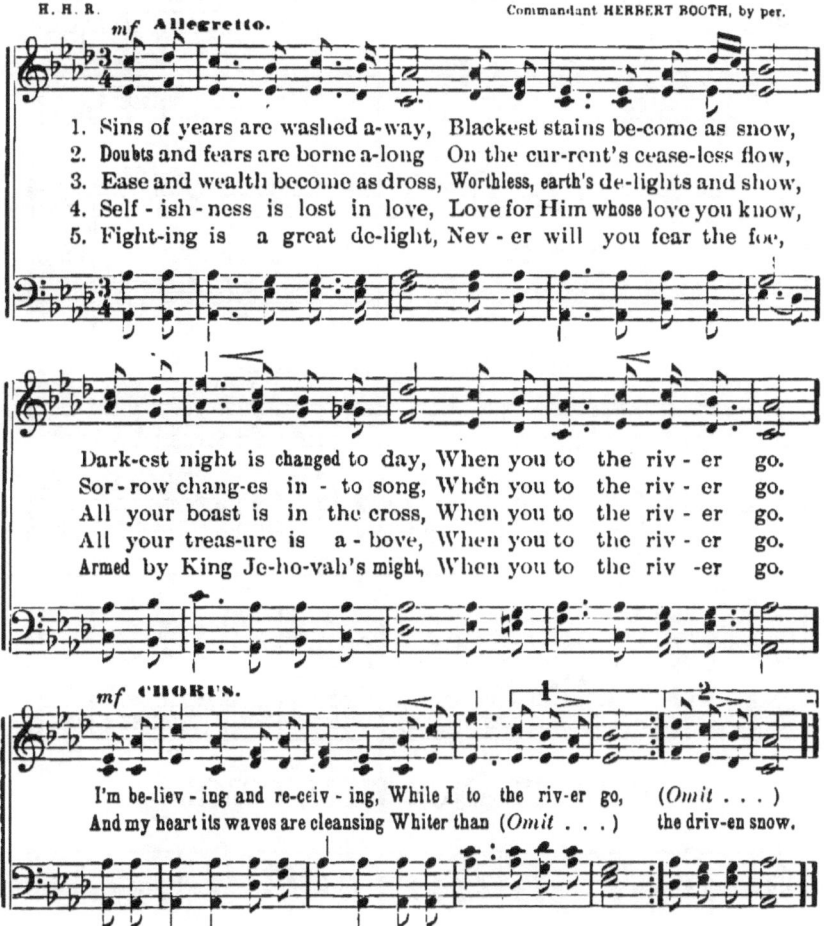

1. Sins of years are washed a-way, Blackest stains be-come as snow,
2. Doubts and fears are borne a-long On the cur-rent's cease-less flow,
3. Ease and wealth become as dross, Worthless, earth's de-lights and show,
4. Self-ish-ness is lost in love, Love for Him whose love you know,
5. Fight-ing is a great de-light, Nev-er will you fear the foe,

Dark-est night is changed to day, When you to the riv-er go.
Sor-row chang-es in-to song, When you to the riv-er go.
All your boast is in the cross, When you to the riv-er go.
All your treas-ure is a-bove, When you to the riv-er go.
Armed by King Je-ho-vah's might, When you to the riv-er go.

CHORUS.

I'm be-liev-ing and re-ceiv-ing, While I to the riv-er go, (Omit...)
And my heart its waves are cleansing Whiter than (Omit...) the driv-en snow.

No. 148. HOW I LOVE THEE.

Tune—"*What a friend we have in Jesus.*"

1 Precious Jesus, how I love Thee,
   Thou hast done so much for me,
Thou hast pardoned my transgressions,
   Thou hast given liberty.
Precious Jesus, I will trust Thee,
   When I'm tempted and oppressed,
Thy great hand will keep me safely,
   Till the storm has o'er me passed.

2 Precious Jesus, Thou hast bought me—
   Bought me with Thy precious blood;
I belong to Thee, dear Saviour,
   I belong to Thee, my God.
I am Thine to do Thy bidding,
   Thine to go where Thou dost send,
Thine to tell to those in darkness,
   Thou art every sinner's friend.

3 Light is found alone in Jesus;
   Christ, our Everlasting Light,
Shine into these hearts, O Saviour,
   Turning darkness into light.
Help us, Lord, to be more watchful
   O'er our thoughts and actions too.
While we keep our eyes on Jesus,
   He will keep us ever true.

By M. LOUISA MILLS, New York.

No. 152. *Music No. 149.*

1 My heavenly home is bright and fair:
Nor pain nor death can enter there;
Its glittering towers the sun outshine
That heavenly mansion shall be mine.

CHORUS.

I'm going home, I'm going home,
I'm going home to die no more;
To die no more, to die no more,
I'm going home to die no more.

2 My Father's house is built on high,
Far, far above the starry sky.
When from this earthly prison free,
That heavenly mansion mine shall be.

3 While here a stranger far from home,
Afflictions waves may round me foam;
Although like Lazarus, sick and poor,
My heavenly mansion is secure.

No. 153. *Music No. 150.*

1 We praise Thee, O God!
 For the Son of Thy love,
 For Jesus who died,
 And is now gone above.

CHORUS.

Hallelujah! Thine the glory,
 Hallelujah! Amen.
Hallelujah! Thine the glory,
 Revive us again.

2 We praise Thee, O God!
 For Thy spirit of light,
Who has shown us our Saviour,
 And scatter'd our night.

3 All glory and praise
 To the Lamb that was slain,
Who has borne all our sins
 And has cleans'd ev'ry stain.

4 Revive us again;
 Fill each heart with Thy love,
May each soul be rekindled
 With fire from above.

No. 154. *Music No. 151.*

1 I saw a happy pilgrim,
 In shining garments clad,
While traveling up the mountain,
 His countenance was glad;
He had no cares nor burdens,
 He'd laid them at the cross,
The blood of Christ, his Saviour,
 Had cleansed him from all dross.

CHORUS.

Then palms of victory,
 Crowns of glory,
Palms of victory,
 We shall wear.

2 The summer sun was shining,
 The sweat was on his brow,
His garments worn and dusty,
 His step seemed very slow,
But he kept pressing onward,
 For he was wending home;
Still shouting as he journeyed,
 Deliverance will come:

3 I saw him in the evening,
 The sun was bending low,
Had overtopped the mountain;
 And reached the vale below;
He saw the golden city,
 His everlasting home,
And shouted loud, Hosannah!
 Deliverance will come.

No. 155. LOST AFTER ALL.

(*Can be sung to tune "After the Ball."*)

1 A little child is kneeling by his mother's chair,
Softly repeating sweet words of prayer
"Dear Loving Jesus, Gentle and Mild
Look down, and bless me, thy little child."
Long kneels the Mother, praying that night,
"God bless my treasure, guide him a-right"
List to his story, weep o'er his fall,
Through his own madness, lost after all.

REFRAIN.

After the days of childhood;
After a Mother's prayer,
After the years of manhood,
Freighted with joys and cares;
After a thousand chances,
After the final call,
Bitter the wail of a spirit;
Lost after all.

2 Changed is the picture, years have swiftly flown,
Sadly the mother waits all alone.
Waits for her darling where does he roam,
Has he forgotten mother and home?
Hark, there's a footstep, surely, 'tis he,
Oh Heaven help her what does she see?
Inside he staggers, one groan. a fall;
Wrecked by the wine cup, lost after all.

3 Farther and farther from his Mother's God,
Wanders he on in sins road so broad,
Till by the window one stormy night.
He finds her waiting lifeless and white;
Vainly the spirit strives for his soul.
Spurning his God he turns to the bowl
Angels in Heaven, weep o'er his fall,
Still unrepentant, lost after all.

Copyright, 1895, by Charlie D. Tillman.

No. 156. THE PRINCE OF MY PEACE.

Words by Rev. W. F. Crafts. Music by W. G. Fischer. By per.

1. I stand all be-wilder'd with wonder, And gaze on the o-cean of love;
2. I struggled and wrestled to win it, The blessing that setteth me free;
3. He laid His hand on me and heal'd me, And bade me be ev-'ry whit whole;
4. The Prince of my peace is now passing, The light of His face is on me;

And o-ver its waves to my spir-it Comes peace, like a heaven-ly dove.
But when I had ceas'd from my strug-gles, His peace Jesus gave un-to me.
I touch'd but the hem of His garment, And glory came thrilling my soul.
But lis-ten, be-lov-ed, He speaketh: "My peace I will give un-to thee."

REFRAIN.
The cross now cov-ers my sins; The past is un-der the blood;
I'm trusting in Je-sus for all; My will is the will of my God.

No. 157. WE'LL WORK TILL JESUS COMES.

Mrs. Elizabeth Mills.

1 O land of rest for thee I sigh,
  When will the moment come,
  When I shall lay my armor by
  And dwell in peace at home?
Chorus.—
  We'll work till Jesus comes,
  We'll work till Jesus comes,
  We'll work till Jesus comes,
  And we'll be gather'd home.

2 No tranquil joys on earth I know,
  No peaceful sheltering dome,
  This world's a wilderness of woe,
  This world is not my home.

3 To Jesus Christ I fled for rest;
  He bade me cease to roam,
  And lean for succor on his breast,
  Till he conduct me home.

4 I sought at once my Saviour's side,
  No more my steps shall roam;
  With Him I'll brave death's chilling tide,
  And reach my heavenly home.

No. 158. SITTING AT THE FEET OF JESUS.

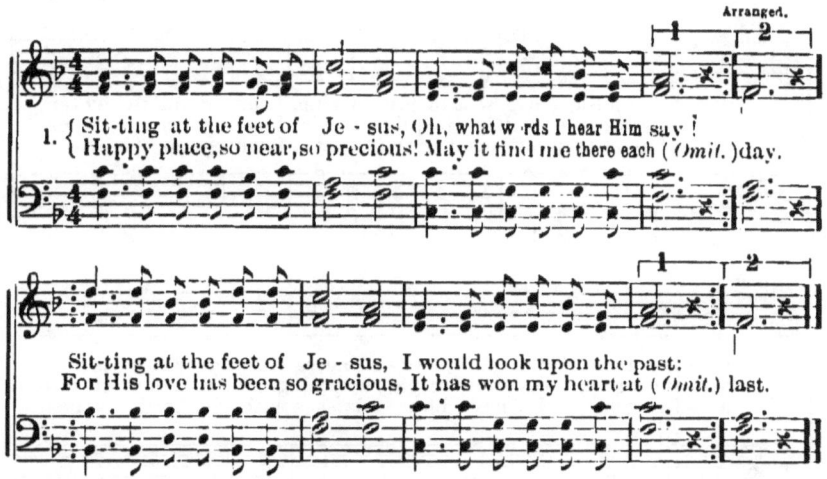

Sit-ting at the feet of Je-sus, Oh, what words I hear Him say!
Happy place, so near, so precious! May it find me there each (Omit.) day.

Sit-ting at the feet of Je-sus, I would look upon the past:
For His love has been so gracious, It has won my heart at (Omit.) last.

2 Sitting at the feet of Jesus,
　Where can mortal be more blest?
There I lay my sins and sorrows,
　And, when weary, find sweet rest;
Sitting at the feet of Jesus,
　There I love to weep and pray,
While I from His fullness gather
　Grace and comfort every day.

3 Bless me, O, my Saviour, bless me,
　As I sit low at Thy feet,
Oh, look down in love upon me,
　Let me see Thy face so sweet;
Give me, Lord, the mind of Jesus,
　Make me holy as He is:
May I prove I've been with Jesus,
　Who is all my righteousness.

No. 159. WE'LL WORK.

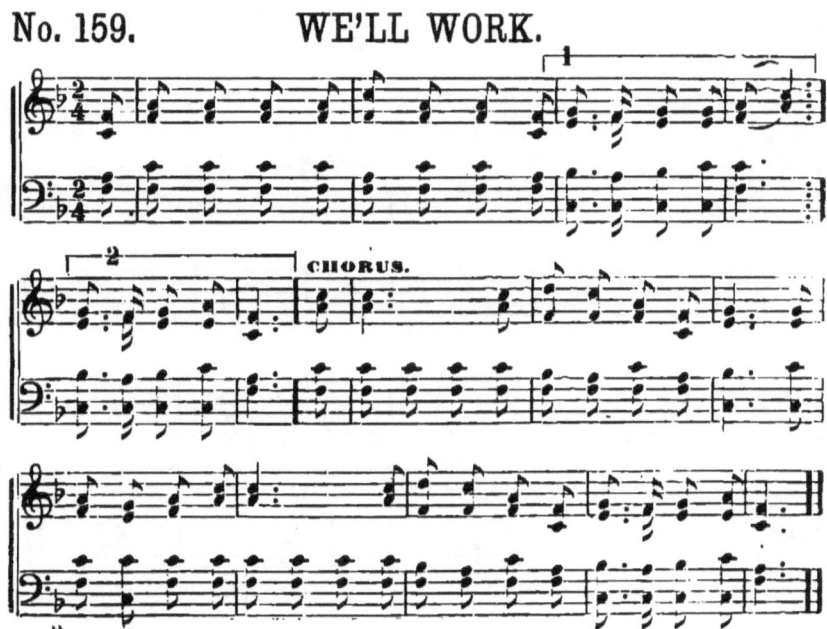

No. 162. Leaning on the Everlasting Arms.

Rev. E. A. HOFFMAN   A. J. SHOWALTER.

1. What a fel-lowship, what a joy divine, Leaning on the ev-er-lasting arms, What a bless-ed-ness, what a peace is mine, Lean-ing on the ev-er-last-ing arms.
2. Oh, how sweet to walk in the pilgrim way, Leaning on the ev-er-lasting arms; Oh, how bright the path grows from day to day, Lean-ing on the ev-er-last-ing arms.
3. What have I to dread, what have I to fear,, Leaning on the ev-er-lasting arms; I have bless-ed peace with my Lord so near, Lean-ing on the ev-er-last-ing arms.

REFRAIN.

Lean-ing, lean-ing, Save and se-cure from all a-larms;
Lean-ing on Je-sus, lean-ing on Jesus,
Lean-ing, lean-ing, Lean-ing on the everlast-ing arms.
Leaning on Jesus, leaning on Jesus,

Copyright, by A. J. Showalter By per.

No. 165. ROOM AT THE FOUNTAIN.

M. J. H. Mrs. M. J. Harris.

1. I heard my loving Saviour say, There's room at the fountain for thee,
2. I came to Him my sins confessed, There was room at the fountain for me,
3. I plunged beneath the crimson tide, There was room at the fountain for me,
4. I found the crimson stream I know, There was room at the fountain for me,

Come wash the stains of sin away, There's room at the fountain for thee.
When I gave up my heart was blest, There's room at the fountain for thee.
And now by faith am sanc-ti-fied, There's room at the fountain for thee.
His blood has washed me white as snow, There's room at the fountain for thee.

CHORUS.

Room, Room, yes there is room, Room at the fountain for thee, for thee;

Room, Room, yes, there is room, There's room at the fountain for thee.

5. He cleansed my heart from inbred sin,
   There was room at the fountain for me,
   And now He keeps me pure within,
   There's room at the fountain for thee.

6. I'll praise Him while He gives me breath,
   There was room at the fountain for me;
   He saved me from an awful death,
   There's room at the fountain for thee.

7. His blood was shed but once for all,
   There was room at the fountain for me;
   Oh, don't reject sweet Mercy's call,
   There's room at the fountain for thee.

8. We'll sing with all the saints above,
   There was room at the fountain for me;
   And praise Him for redeeming love,
   There's room at the fountain for thee.

Copyright, 1897, by Mrs. M. J. Harris.

No. 166. DON'T YOU WANT TO BE THERE?

E. R. LATTA. JNO. R. BRYANT

SEMI-CHORUS.

1. There's a land of wondrous beau-ty! Don't you want to be there?
2. There's a land of deathless pleas-ure, Don't you want to be there?
3. There's a land with cli-mate ver-nal! Don't you want to be there?
4. There's a land where saints are dwelling, Don't you want to be there?

SEMI-CHORUS.

'Tis the price of Chris-tian du-ty—Don't you want to be there?
And of ev-er-last-ing treas-ure—Don't you want to be there?
'Tis the realm of life e-ter-nal—Don't you want to be there?
They the love of Christ are tell-ing! Don't you want to be there?

CHORUS.

How sweet 'twill be a-round His throne, To sing His praise with loved ones gone For-ev-er to a-bide, In the heav-en-ly Je-ru-sa-lem Where we shall know as we are known, Up-on the oth-er side.

Copyright, 1895, by Charlie D. Tillman

No. 167. PRAISE HIM, HALLELUJAH!

Mrs. ADALINE H. BEERY.   Arr. by F. McD. H.

1. I learned a precious secret, Low down at Jesus' feet;
2. For once I was in darkness, And evil pressed me round;
3. No matter how you've wronged Him, Tho' steeped in wickedness;

Cho.—Oh, praise Him, hallelujah! For love so full and free; O

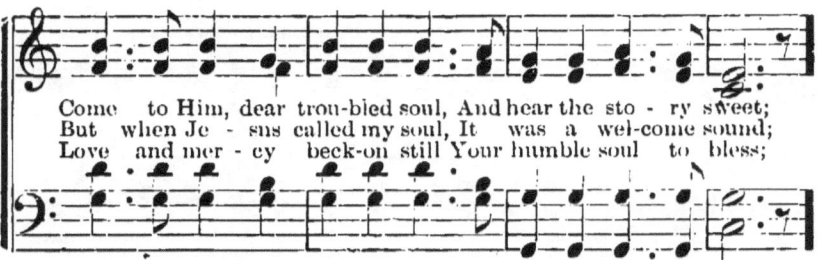

Come to Him, dear troubled soul, And hear the story sweet;
But when Jesus called my soul, It was a welcome sound;
Love and mercy beckon still Your humble soul to bless;

Lamb of God, who saves my soul, All praise I give to Thee;

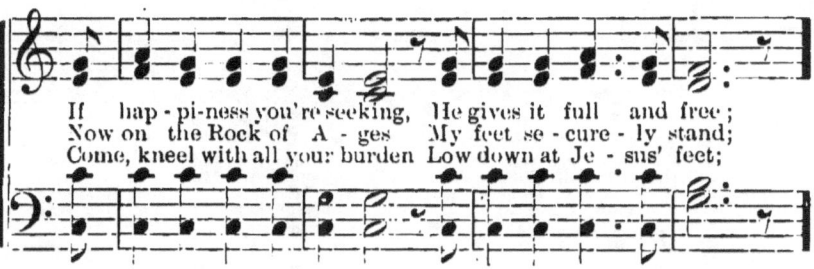

If happiness you're seeking, He gives it full and free;
Now on the Rock of Ages My feet securely stand;
Come, kneel with all your burden Low down at Jesus' feet;

Upon the Rock of Ages My feet securely stand;

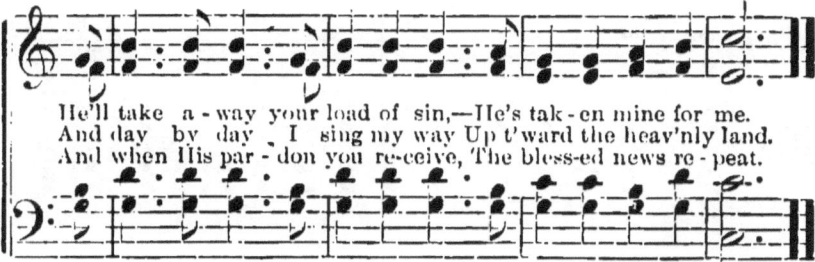

He'll take away your load of sin,—He's taken mine for me.
And day by day I sing my way Up t'ward the heav'nly land.
And when His pardon you receive, The blessed news repeat.

And day by day I sing my way Up t'ward the heav'nly land.

Copyright 1892, by F. McD. Hunter.

No. 171. GO YE INTO ALL THE WORLD.

JESSIE H. BROWN.   J. H. FILLMORE.

1. "Go ye in-to all the world!" 'Tis the lov-ing Lord's command;
2. Go ye to the souls that mourn, With the gracious gos-pel call;
3. Go ye to the souls that grope, Seeking light and find-ing none;

Let His ban-ner be un-furled O-ver ev-'ry land.
Tell how Christ their griefs has borne—How He died for all.
Tell them of the Christian's hope, Tell what Christ has done.

CHORUS

Go ye, go ye, Preach the gospel to ev-'ry creature,
Go ye in-to all the world, into all the world, Preach to ev-'ry creature,

Go ye, go ye, I am with you al - way.
Go ye in-to all the world, into all the world, I am with you al - way.

Copyright, 1896, by Fillmore Bros.

No. 172.   JUST THE SAME TO-DAY.

See 44, in The Revival, No. 1, for Music and Chorus.

1 Have you ever heard the story
    How our Lord before He died
Laid His blessed hands in healing
    Upon all who to Him cried,
How the sick and all oppressed ones
    He rejoicing sent away?
This He claims to do, beloved,
    And He's just the same to-day.

2 Have you ever heard the story
    Of the Pentecostal day,
When the Holy Ghost descended,
    How He had the right of way?
And with cloven tongues of fire
    Inbred sin was swept away?
Oh, I'm glad, so glad to tell you
    He is just the same to-day.

3 Have you ever heard the promise
    That our risen Lord should come
Down to earth again and gather
    All His chosen people home?
Oh, He says He's surely coming,
    We must watch as well as pray;
God declares His word unchanging,
    He is just the same to-day.

WAITING FOR HIS COMING. Concluded.

All His praises we will sing, We are wait - - ing
hal - le - lujah, We are waiting, we are waiting
for the com - - ing Of our Sav - iour, Lord and King.
for the coming, blessed coming

No. 174.   HE SAVES.

F. McD. H., arr.

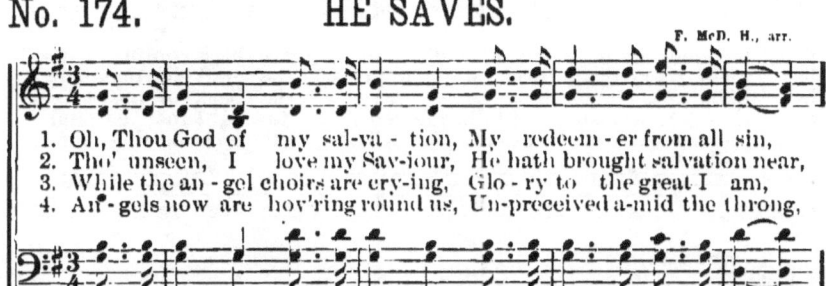

1. Oh, Thou God of my sal-va - tion, My redeem - er from all sin,
2. Tho' unseen, I love my Sav-iour, He hath brought salvation near,
3. While the an - gel choirs are cry-ing, Glo - ry to the great I am,
4. An - gels now are hov'ring round us, Un-preceived a-mid the throng,

Cho.—Hal-le-lu - jah, hal - le - lu - jah, Hal - le - lu - jah, Je-sus saves,

CHORUS. D. C.

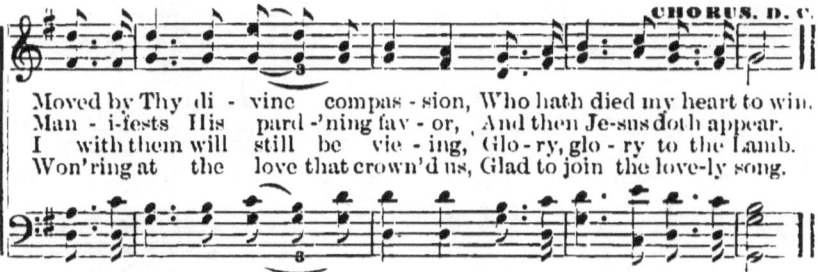

Moved by Thy di - vine compas - sion, Who hath died my heart to win.
Man - i-fests His pard-'ning fav - or, And then Je-sus doth appear.
I with them will still be vie - ing, Glo - ry, glo - ry to the Lamb.
Won'ring at the love that crown'd us, Glad to join the love-ly song.

Yes, He saves me just at this mo-ment, Hal - le - lu - jah, Je-sus saves.

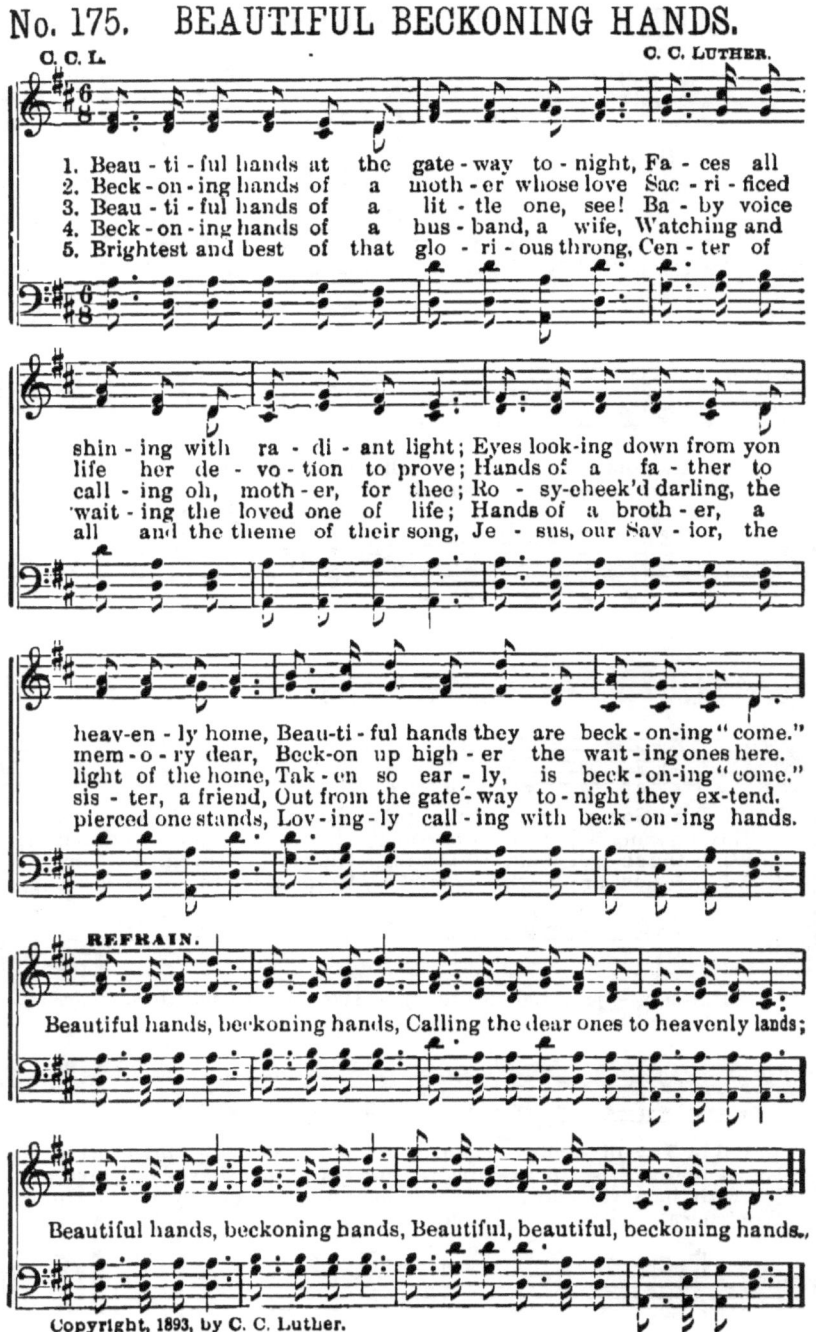

No. 176. THE RESURRECTION.

G. R. Street. By per. of A. S. Kieffer.

CALVARY. Concluded.

No. 181. I'LL GO WITH HIM.

GEO. W. COLLINS. Arr. for This Work.

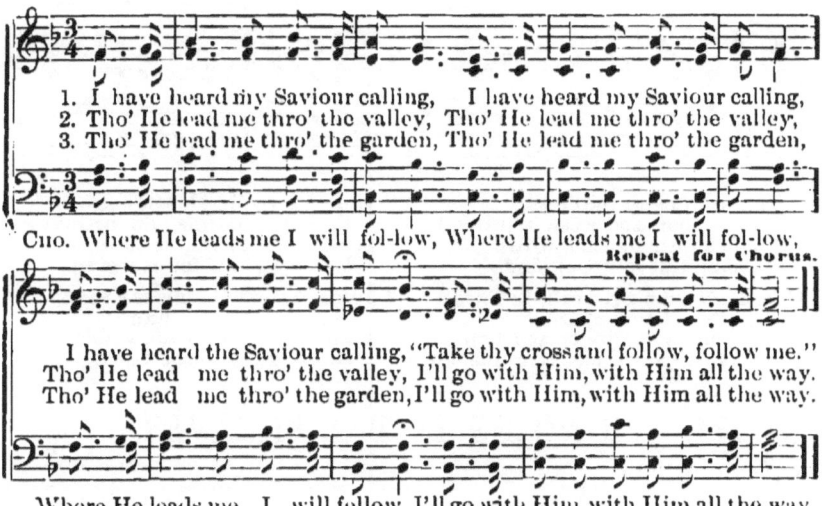

1. I have heard my Saviour calling, I have heard my Saviour calling,
2. Tho' He lead me thro' the valley, Tho' He lead me thro' the valley,
3. Tho' He lead me thro' the garden, Tho' He lead me thro' the garden,

Cho. Where He leads me I will fol-low, Where He leads me I will fol-low,
Repeat for Chorus.

I have heard the Saviour calling, "Take thy cross and follow, follow me."
Tho' He lead me thro' the valley, I'll go with Him, with Him all the way.
Tho' He lead me thro' the garden, I'll go with Him, with Him all the way.

Where He leads me I will follow, I'll go with Him, with Him all the way.
Copyright, 1894, by Jno. R. Bryant.

4 :Tho' the path be dark and dreary,:
 I'll go with Him, with Him all the way.
5 :Tho' He lead me to the conflict,:
 I'll go with Him, with Him all the way.
6 :Tho' He lead thro' fiery trials,:
 I'll go with Him, with Him all the way.

7 :I will follow on to know Him,:
 He's my Saviour, Saviour, Brother, Friend.
8 :He will give me grace and glory,:
 He will keep me, keep me all the way.
9 :Oh, 'tis sweet to follow Jesus,:
 And be with Him, with Him all the way.

No. 182. "OLD TIME RELIGION."

Arr. by CHARLIE TILLMAN.

Cho. 'Tis the old time re-lig-ion, 'Tis the old time religion, 'Tis the old time re-
1. It was good for our mothers, It was good for our mothers, It was good for our
2. Makes me love ev'ry-body, Makes me love ev-'rybody, Makes me love ev'ry-
3. It has sav-ed our fa-thers, It has sav-ed our fathers, It has sav-ed our

li-gion, It's good enough for me.
mothers, It's good enough for me.
bod-y, It's good enough for me.
fathers, It's good enough for me.

4 :It was good for the Prophet Daniel,:
 It's good enough for me.
5 :It was good for the Hebrew Children,:
 It's good enough for me.
6 :It was tried in the fiery furnace,:
 It's good enough for me.
7 :It was good for Paul and Silas,:
 It's good enough for me.
8 :It will do when I am dying,:
 It's good enough for me.
9 :It will take us all to heaven,:
 It's good enough for me.

Copyright, 1891, by Charlie D. Tillman.

No. 183. I AM COMING.

W. G. FISCHER.

1 I am coming to the cross;
  I am poor, and weak and blind;
  I am counting all but dross.
  I shall full salvation find.

Cho. I am trusting, Lord, in Thee,
  Dear Lamb of Calvary;
  Humbly at Thy cross I bow,
  Jesus, saves me, saves me now.

2 Here I give my all to Thee,
  Friends and time, and earthly store:
  Soul and body, Thine to be,—
  Wholly Thine for evermore.

3 Jesus comes! He fills my soul!
  Perfected in love I am;
  I am every whit made whole;
  Glory, glory to the Lamb.

No. 184. BRINGING IN THE SHEAVES.

From "Songs of Glory." GEO. A. MINOR.

1 Sowing in the morning, sowing seeds of kindness,
  Sowing in the noontide, and the dewy eves;
  Waiting for the harvest, and the time of reaping,
  We shall come rejoicing, bringing in the sheaves.

Cho.—Bringing in the sheaves, bringing in the sheaves,
  We shall come rejoicing, bringing in the sheaves.

2 Sowing in the sunshine, sowing in the shadows,
  Fearing neither clouds nor winter's chilling breeze;
  By and by the harvest, and the labor ended,
  We shall come rejoicing, bringing in the sheaves.

3 Go then, ever weeping, sowing for the Master,
  Though the loss sustained our spirit often grieves;
  When our weeping's over, He will bid us welcome,
  We shall come rejoicing, bringing in the sheaves,

No. 188. **BEAUTIFUL POOL.**

COWPER.
WILL M. WALLER.
Har. by CHARLIE D. TILLMAN.

1. There is a fount-ain filled with blood, Drawn from Immanuel's veins; And sin-ners plunged be-neath that flood, Lose all their guil-ty stains. Go wash in that beau-ti-ful
2. The dy-ing thief re-joiced to see That fount-ain in his day; And there may I, tho' vile as he, Wash all my sins a-way.

D. S. A fount-ain of life for all man-kind, Go

Fine. CHORUS.

wash in that beau-ti-ful pool.

D. S.

pool (beautiful pool), Go wash in that beau-ti-ful pool (beautiful pool);

Copyright, 1892, by Charlie D. Tillman.

3 Dear dying Lamb, Thy precious blood
  Shall never lose its power,
Till all the ransomed church of God
  Be saved to sin no more.

4 E'er since by faith, I saw the stream
  Thy flowing wounds supply.

Redeeming love has been my theme,
  And shall be till I die.

5 Then in a nobler, sweeter song,
  I'll sing Thy power to save,
When this poor lisping, stamm'ring tongue
  Lies silent in the grave.

No. 189. A MOTHER'S PLEA.

Dedicated to Sherrard Beatty, of The Rescue Mission, Cincinnati, O., by one of the Converts.

HUGH MULHOLLAND.   EDW. S. FOGG.

SOLO or DUET.

1. Dear friends, if to night, Midst the rain and the sleet, A poor drunken boy On the street you should meet, Remember his mother is praying for him. O tell him of Jesus, And take my boy in!
2. O tell him of Jesus, That the dear boy may know, Though his sins be as scarlet, He'll make them as snow. Have him kneel down in prayer, As with mother he knelt In the old house at home, Where no sorrow was felt.
3. Send back to me, With a heart full of glee, The boy that knelt At his dear mother's knee. She longs to hear him tell Jesus freed him from sin, And has guided him home By the prayers said within.

CHORUS.

He's some mother's boy; No matter who he be, True love nev-er falters At a dear mother's plea.

Copyright

No 190. THE SPIRIT IS CALLING.

L. E. JONES.   CHARLIE D. TILLMAN.

1. The Spirit is calling, oh, do not delay, But turn, quickly turn from the danger-fraught way; There's safety nowhere but in Jesus the Lord, So come to Him now and believe in His word.
2. The Spirit is calling, in tenderest voice, Oh, hasten today and your heart shall rejoice, For with the Redeemer, the tried and oppressed, Shall find a blest haven of comfort and rest.
3. The Spirit is calling, oh, do not say no, Escape from a service that's freighted with woe; Just come as you are to the foot of the throne And Christ will accept you and make you His own.

CHORUS.

The Spirit is calling, is calling, Is tenderly calling; . . The Spirit is calling, . . Is calling for calling for thee, Is tenderly calling, "Oh, come unto me;" The Spirit is calling, is calling for thee, Is calling, is calling for

Copyright, 1896, by Charlie D. Tillman.

2 Jesus calls in sweet compassion;
  Jesus will save, yes, Jesus will save;
 Don't reject the invitation;
  Jesus will save, yes, Jesus will save;
 He will set your spirit free,
  Rise forthwith, He calleth thee;
 Brother hear the invitation,
  Jesus will save, yes, Jesus will save.

3 Hear that dying intercession,
  Jesus will save, yes, Jesus will save;
 He will pardon your transgression,
  Jesus will save, yes, Jesus will save;
 Come, ye weary souls, to me,
  Rise forthwith, He calleth thee,
 Brother hear the invitation,
  Jesus will save, yes, Jesus will save

No. 192. JESUS IS ABLE TO SAVE.

MAGGIE E. GREGORY.   CHAS. H. GABRIEL.

1. Jesus is able to save us from sin, And cleanse us from each guilty stain,
2. Jesus is a-ble to save us from sin, If we will repent and be-lieve;
3. Jesus will save you, my brother, this hour, Oh, will you not prove Him and see?

None who in penitence seek His dear face, Have ever sought it in vain.
All who come trusting His mercy and grace, Shall perfect cleansing receive.
Come! He will pardon and cleanse you from sin, For oh, He saved even me.

CHORUS

Jesus is a-ble to save us from sin; A - ble, yes, a - ble!
Tho' our transgressions be many and deep,
Yes, He is a-ble to pardon and save, And al-so a-ble to keep.

Copyright, 1896, by Charlie D. Tillman.

No. 196. When the Roll is Called up Yonder.

No. 198. LET THE SUNSHINE IN.

ADA BLENKHORN.
CHAS. H. GABRIEL.

1. Do you fear the foe will in the conflict win? Is it dark without you,—darker still within? Clear the darkened windows, open wide the door, Let a little sunshine in.
2. Does your faith grow fainter in the cause you love? Are your pray's unanswer'd by your God above? Clear the darkened windows, open wide the door, Let a little sunshine in.
3. Would you go rejoicing on the upward way, Knowing naught of darkness,—dwelling in the day? Clear the darkened windows, open wide the door, Let a little sunshine in.

CHORUS.

Let the blessed sunshine in, . . Let the blessed sunshine in; . . Clear the darken'd windows, open wide the door, Let a little sunshine in.

Copyright 1890, by Chas. H. Gabriel.

No. 200. LIFE'S RAILWAY TO HEAVEN.

Respectfully dedicated to the railroad men.

M. E. ABBEY.
SOLO OR DUET.
Tempo ad lib.
CHARLIE D. TILLMAN.

1. Life is like a mountain railroad, With an engineer that's brave;
2. You will roll up grades of trial; You will cross the bridge of strife;
3. You will often find obstructions; Look for storms of wind and rain;
4. As you roll across the trestle, Spanning Jordan's swelling tide,

We must make the run successful, From the cradle to the grave;
See that Christ is your conductor On this lightning train of life;
On a fill, or curve, or trestle, They will almost ditch your train;
You be-hold the Union Depot Into which your train will glide;

Watch the curves, the fills, the tunnels; Never falter, never quail;
Always mindful of obstruction, Do your du-ty, never fail;
Put your trust alone in Je-sus; Nev-er fal-ter, never fail;
There you'll meet the Superintendant, God the Father, God the Son,

Rit.

Keep your hand upon the throttle, And your eye upon the rail.
Keep your hand upon the throttle, And your eye upon the rail.
Keep your hand upon the throttle, And your eye upon the rail.
With the hearty, joyous plaudit, "Wea-ry pilgrim, welcome home."

Copyright, 1891, by Charlie D. Tillman.

LIFE'S RAILWAY TO HEAVEN. Concluded.

CHORUS.

Blessed Savior, thou wilt guide us Till we reach that blissful shore;
Where the an-gels wait to join us In thy praise for evermore.

No. 201.   I DO BELIEVE. C. M.

REV. CHARLES WESLEY.   Unknown.

1. Fath-er, I stretch my hands to thee, No oth-er help I know;
2. What did thine on-ly Son endure, Be-fore I drew my breath;
3. O Jesus, could I this believe, I now should feel thy pow'r;
4. Auth-or of faith, to thee I lift My weary, long-ing eyes;

CHO. I do be-lieve, I now believe, That Jesus died for me;

If thou withdraw thyself from me, Ah, whither shall I go?
What pain, what labor to se-cure My soul from end-less death?
And all my wants thou wouldst relieve, In this ac-cept-ed hour.
Oh, let me now re-ceive that gift; My soul without it dies.

And thro' his blood, his precious blood, I shall from sin be free.

No. 202. THE PENITENT'S PLEA.

B. H. B.   COMMANDANT BOOTH

DUET

1. Saviour, hear me while before Thy feet I the record of my sins repeat, Stained with guilt, myself abhorring, Filled with grief, my soul out-pouring, Canst Thou still in mercy think of me, Stoop to
2. Back with all the guilt my spirit bears, Past the haunting memories of years, Self and shame and fear despising, Foes and taunting fiends surprising, Saviour, to Thy cross I press my way, And a
3. Yet why should I fear, hast Thou not died That no seeking soul should be denied? To that heart its sins confessing, Canst Thou fail to give a blessing? By the love and pity Thou hast shown, By the
4. All the rivers of Thy grace I claim, Over ev'ry promise write my name; As I am I come believing, As Thou art Thou dost, receiving, Bid me rise a freed and pardoned slave; Master

By permission.

THE PENITENT'S PLEA. Concluded.

No. 203. STEP OUT ON THE PROMISE.

The Highway.   E. F. Miller.

1. O mourner in Zi-on, how blessed art thou, For Jesus is waiting to comfort you now; Fear not to rely on the word of thy God. Step out on the promise, get under the blood.
2. Oh, ye that are hungry and thirsty rejoice; For ye shall be filled; do you hear that sweet voice Inviting now to the banquet of God? Step out on the promise, get under the blood.
3. Who sighs for a heart from iniquity free? Oh, poor troubled soul! there's a promise for thee; There's rest, weary one, in the bosom of God. Step out on the promise, get under the blood.
4. The promise don't save, tho' the promise is true; 'Tis the blood we get under, that cleanses us through: It cleanses me now, hallelujah to God. I rest on the promise, I'm under the blood.

Copyright, 1884, by E. F. Miller.

204.

1 Sweet hour of prayer, sweet hour of prayer,
That calls me from a world of care,
And bids me at my Father's throne
Make all my wants and wishes known!
In seasons of distress and grief
My soul has often found relief,
And oft escaped the tempter's snare
By thy return, sweet hour of prayer.

2 Sweet hour of prayer, sweet hour of prayer,
Thy wings shall my petition bear
To Him, whose truth and faithfulness
Engage the waiting soul to bless:
And since He bids me seek His face,
Believe His word, and trust His grace,
I'll cast on Him my every care,
And wait for thee, sweet hour of prayer.

No. 205. HOW FIRM A FOUNDATION. 11s.

GEORGE KEITH.

1. How firm a foundation, ye saints of the Lord, Is laid for your faith in his ex-cellent word! What more can he say than to you he hath said, You who un-to Je-sus for refuge have fled?
2. In ev-'ry condition—in sickness, in health; In pov-er-ty's vale, or a-bounding in wealth; At home and a-broad; on the land, on the sea—"As thy days may demand, shall thy strength ever be.
3. "Fear not; I am with thee; oh, be not dismayed! I, I am thy God, and will still give thee aid; I'll strengthen thee, help thee, and cause thee to stand, Up-held by my righteous, omnipo-tent hand.

4 "When through the deep waters I call thee to go,
The rivers of woe shall not thee overflow;
For I will be with thee, thy troubles to bless,
And sanctify to thee thy deepest distress.

5 "When through fiery trials thy pathway shall lie,
My grace, all-sufficient, shall be thy supply:
The flame shall not hurt thee—I only design
Thy dross to consume, and thy gold to refine.

6 "E'en down to old age, all my people shall prove
My sovereign, eternal, unchangeable love;
And when hoary hairs shall their temples adorn,
Like lambs they shall still in my bosom be borne.

7 "The soul that on Jesus still leans for repose,
I will not, I *will* not, desert to his foes;
That soul, though all hell should endeavor to shake,
I'll never, *no, never*, NO, NEVER forsake."

No. 208. SATISFIED WITH JESUS.

E. E. HEWITT.   WM. J. KIRKPATRICK.

1. I am sat-is-fied with Je-sus, He is all in all to me;
2. Sweetly sat-is-fied with Je-sus, Not with a-ny hope be-side,
3. Ev-er sat-is-fied with Je-sus, When the summer roses bloom,
4. I am sat-is-fied with Je-sus, May His grace a-bun-dant be,

In my heart His love is springing Like a fount-ain glad and free.
For the spir-it's thirst and hunger, No where else can be supplied.
When the win-try snows are drifting, Then His smile will light the gloom.
All His ho-ly will ac-com-plish, Till He's sat-is-fied with me.

There is "now no con-dem-na-tion" To a soul be-neath the flow
Not with a-ny past at-tain-ment, A-ny good my hands may do,
He has prom-ised to be with me, And His love is joy di-vine,
When—all praise to His sal-va-tion,—Gates of pearl shall o-pen wide,

D. S. In my heart His love is spring-ing Like a fount-ain glad and free;

Of the stream from Cal-vary's mountain Cleansing whiter than the snow.
On-ly Je-sus, precious Saviour, Gives me peace, a-bid-ing, true.
While I hear the gen-tle whis-per, I am His, and He is mine.
I shall wake up in His like-ness, There, for-ev-er, "sat-is-fied."

And I know that Je-sus loves me, For He gave Him-self for me."

Copyright, 1894, by W. J. Kirkpatrick.

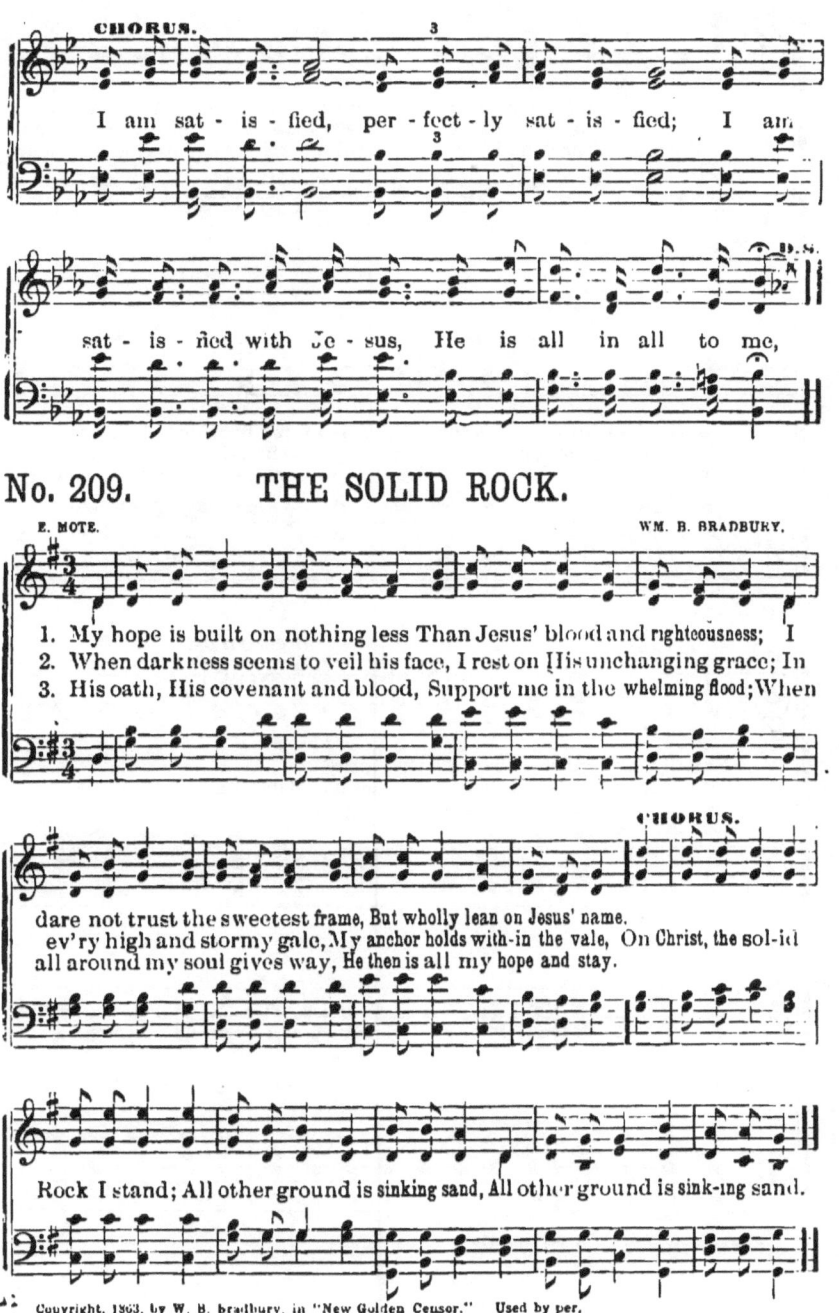

VOTE AS YOU PRAY. Concluded.

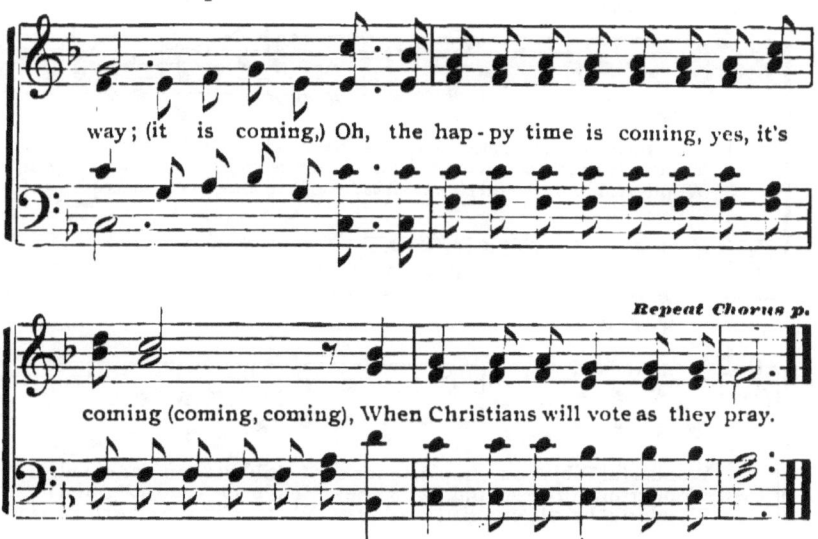

way; (it is coming,) Oh, the hap-py time is coming, yes, it's

Repeat Chorus p.

coming (coming, coming), When Christians will vote as they pray.

No. 211.   I'LL BE THERE TO VOTE.

Arr. by R. E. Hudson.
Re-arr. by Charlie D. Tillman.

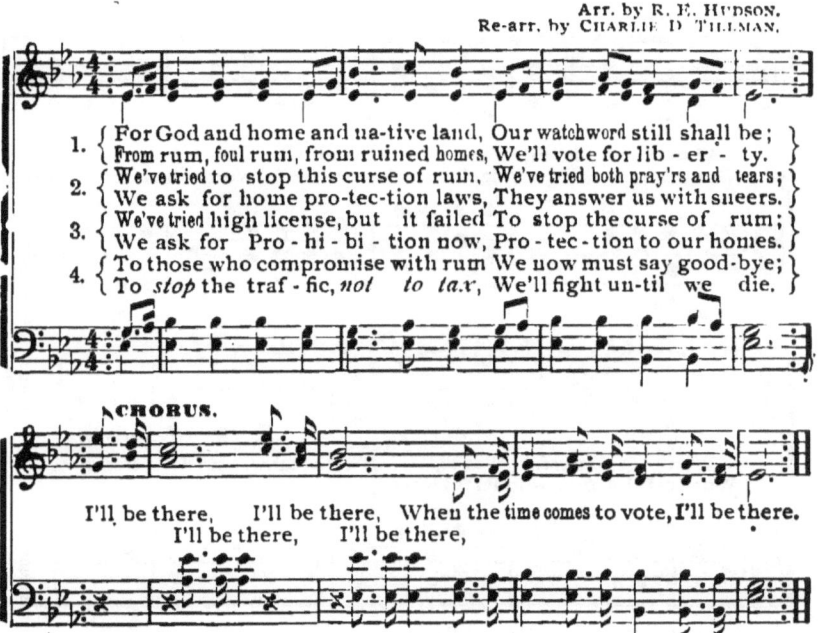

1. { For God and home and na-tive land, Our watchword still shall be;
     From rum, foul rum, from ruined homes, We'll vote for lib-er-ty. }
2. { We've tried to stop this curse of rum, We've tried both pray'rs and tears;
     We ask for home pro-tec-tion laws, They answer us with sneers. }
3. { We've tried high license, but it failed To stop the curse of rum;
     We ask for Pro-hi-bi-tion now, Pro-tec-tion to our homes. }
4. { To those who compromise with rum We now must say good-bye;
     To *stop* the traf-fic, *not to tax*, We'll fight un-til we die. }

CHORUS.

I'll be there, I'll be there, When the time comes to vote, I'll be there.
I'll be there, I'll be there,

No. 213. JESUS, I MY CROSS HAVE TAKEN.

HENRY F. LYTE.   MOZART.

1. Je-sus, I my cross have taken, All to leave and follow thee;
2. Let the world despise, forsake me, They have left my Savior, too;
3. Go, then, earthly fame and treasure! Come, disaster, scorn and pain!

Na-ked, poor, despised, forsaken, Thou from hence my all shalt be;
Human hearts and looks deceive me, Thou art not, like man, untrue;
In thy service, pain is pleasure; With thy fa-vor, loss is gain.

Perish ev-'ry fond ambi-tion, All I've sought and hoped and known;
And, while thou shalt smile upon me, God of wisdom, love and might,
I have called thee, "Abba, Father," I have stayed my heart on thee;

Yet how rich is my condition, God and heav'n are still my own.
Foes may hate and friends may shun me, Show thy face and all is bright.
Storms may howl and clouds may gather, All must work for good to me.

No. 217. COME, EVERY SOUL.

1 Come, every soul by sin oppressed,
  There's mercy with the Lord,
And He will surely give you rest,
  By trusting in His word.
Cho.—Only trust Him, only trust Him,
    Only trust Him now;
  He will save you, He will save you,
    He will save you now.

2 For Jesus shed His precious blood
  Rich blessings to bestow;
Plunge now into the crimson tide
  That washes white as snow.
Cho.—Come to Jesus, come to Jesus,
    Come to Jesus now;
  He will save you, He will save you,
    He will save you now.

3 O Jesus, blessed Jesus, dear,
  I'm coming now to Thee,
Since Thou hast made the way so clear
  And full salvation free.
Cho.—I will trust Him, I will trust Him,
    I will trust Him now;
  He will save me, He will save me,
    He will save me now.

No. 223. STANDING ON THE PROMISES.

R. K. C.   R. KELSO CARTER.

1. Standing on the promis-es of Christ my King, Thro' e-ter-nal a-ges let His prais-es ring, Glo-ry in the high-est, I will shout and sing, Standing on the promis-es of God.
2. Standing on the promis-es that can-not fail, When the howl-ing storms of doubt and fear assail, By the liv-ing Word of God, I shall pre-vail, Standing on the promis-es of God.
3. Standing on the promis-es I now can see, Per-fect, pres-ent cleansing in the blood for me; Stand-ing in the lib-er-ty where Christ makes free, Standing on the promis-es of God.
4. Standing on the promis-es of Christ the Lord, Bound to Him e-ter-nal-ly by love's strong cord, O-ver-com-ing dai-ly with the Spir-it's sword, Standing on the promis-es of God.
5. Standing on the promis-es I can-not fall, Listening ev-'ry moment to the Spir-it's call, Rest-ing in my Sav-iour, as my all in all, Standing on the promis-es of God.

CHORUS.

Stand - ing, stand - ing, Standing on the promis-es of God, my Sav-iour, Standing on the promise, Standing on the promise,

Stand - ing, stand - ing, I'm standing on the promises of God.
Standing on the promise, Standing on the promise,

Copyright, 1886, by John J. Hood.

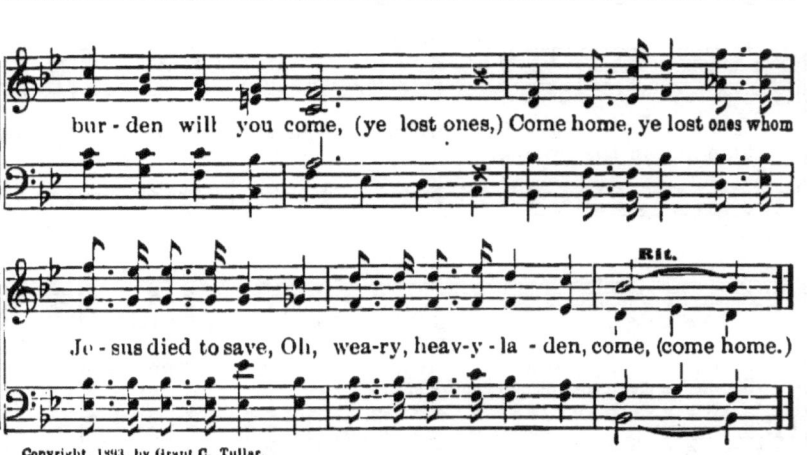

Every Hour I Need Thy Blessing. Concluded.

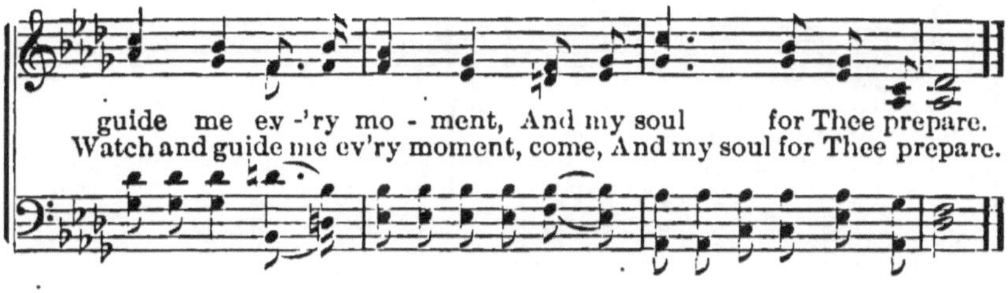

guide me ev-'ry mo - ment, And my soul for Thee prepare.
Watch and guide me ev'ry moment, come, And my soul for Thee prepare.

No. 227.   RESCUE THE PERISHING.

F. J. CROSBY.   W. H. DOANE.

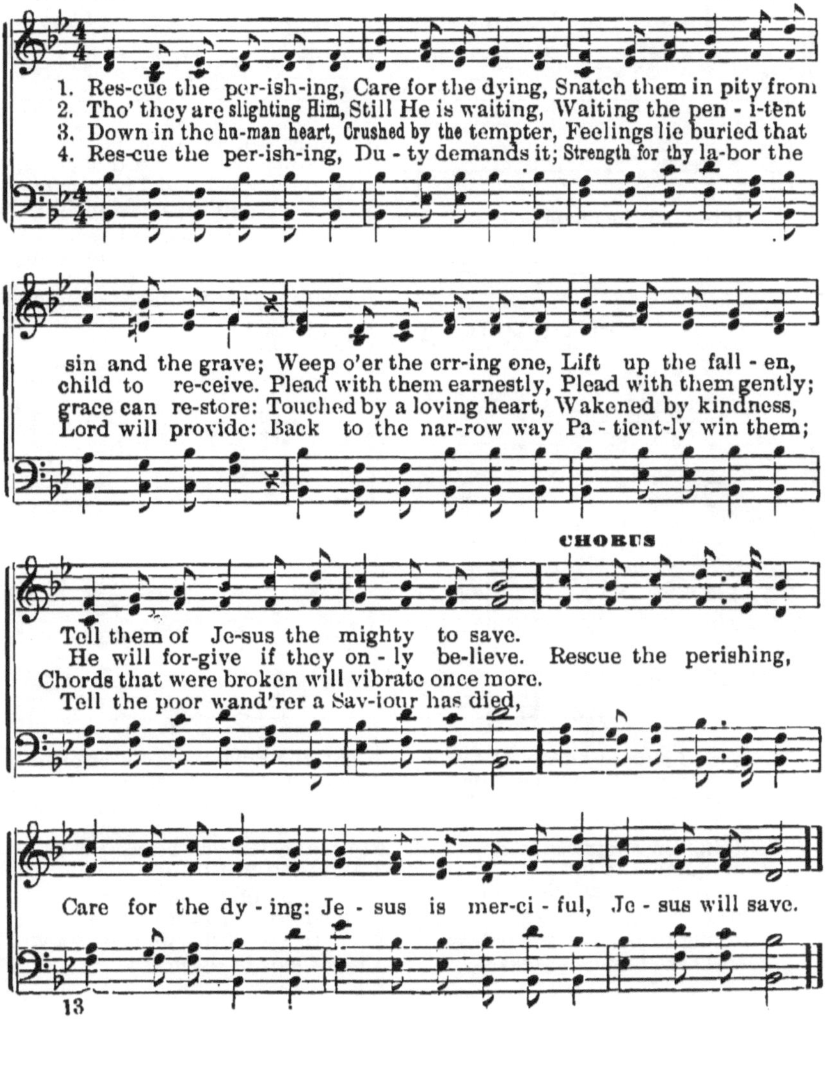

1. Res-cue the per-ish-ing, Care for the dying, Snatch them in pity from
2. Tho' they are slighting Him, Still He is waiting, Waiting the pen - i-tent
3. Down in the hu-man heart, Crushed by the tempter, Feelings lie buried that
4. Res-cue the per-ish-ing, Du - ty demands it; Strength for thy la-bor the

sin and the grave; Weep o'er the err-ing one, Lift up the fall - en,
child to re-ceive. Plead with them earnestly, Plead with them gently;
grace can re-store: Touched by a loving heart, Wakened by kindness,
Lord will provide: Back to the nar-row way Pa - tient-ly win them;

CHORUS

Tell them of Je-sus the mighty to save.
He will for-give if they on - ly be-lieve. Rescue the perishing,
Chords that were broken will vibrate once more.
Tell the poor wand'rer a Sav-iour has died,

Care for the dy - ing: Je - sus is mer-ci - ful, Je - sus will save.

No. 228. NOTHING BUT THE BLOOD OF JESUS.

R. L. — Music by R. LOWRY. By per.

1. What can wash away my sin? Nothing but the blood of Jesus;
   What can make me whole again? Nothing but the blood of Jesus.

2. For my pardon this I see— Nothing but the blood of Jesus;
   For my cleansing, this my plea,— Nothing but the blood of Jesus.

CHORUS.
Oh, precious is the flow That makes me white as snow; No other Fount I know, Nothing but the blood of Jesus.

3 Nothing can for sin atone,
  Nothing but the blood of Jesus;
  Naught of good that I have done,
  Nothing but the blood of Jesus.

4 This is all my hope and peace—
  Nothing but the blood of Jesus;
  This is all my righteousness—
  Nothing but the blood of Jesus.

No. 229. THERE IS A FOUNTAIN.

COWPER. — Unknown.

1 There is a fountain filled with blood
  Drawn from Immanuel's veins,
  And sinners plunged beneath that flood
  Lose all their guilty stains.

  The dying thief rejoiced to see
  That fountain in his day;
  And there have I, as vile as he,
  Washed all my sins away.

2 Dear dying Lamb, Thy precious blood
  Shall never lose its power,
  Till all the ransomed Church of God
  Be saved to sin no more.

4 E'er since by faith I saw the stream
  Thy flowing wounds supply,
  Redeeming love has been my theme,
  And shall be till I die.

5. Then in a nobler, sweeter song,
   I'll sing Thy power to save,
   When this poor lisping, stammering tongue
   Lies silent in the grave.

No. 331. FORWARD LEAGUERS.

DEDICATED TO EPWORTH LEAGUES.

Rev. T. W. Barker. Edw. S. Fogg.

1. Come ye Epworth band, Forward ev'ry man, Let us take the land
2. Marching on we go, Let us meet the foe, Faith in Christ we know
3. We are leaguers strong, Forward is our song, As we march a-long
4. When our work is done, And our race is run, And the bat-tle won

for the Lord; Keep your armor bright, Stand firm for the right,
must prevail; Walk-ing in the light, Shield and banner bright,
on the way; Let us shout and sing, And the sin-ner bring,
here be-low; We will climb the heights, And en-joy delights,

CHORUS.

With your eyes upon his ho-ly word.
Fighting for the right we can not fail. Forward leaguers, rally round the
Unto Christ, our King, as we all pray.
And as we are known we all shall know.

Cornet.

standard Epworth-Leaguers let us march a-long; Forward leaguers,

shout a-loud ho-san-na, Christ is Captain and will lead us on.

Copyright 1895, by Fogg and Barker.

No. 232. GLORY TO HIS NAME.

E. A. HOFFMAN.   REV. J. H. STOCKTON, By per.

1. Down at the cross where the Sav-ior died, Down where for cleans-ing from sin I cried, There to my heart was the blood ap-plied, Glo-ry to his name!
2. I am so won-drous-ly saved from sin, Je-sus so sweet-ly a-bides with-in, Saves me each mo-ment, and keeps me clean; Glo-ry to his name!
3. Come to this foun-tain, so rich and sweet; Cast thy poor soul at the Sav-ior's feet; Plunge in to-day, and be made com-plete, Glo-ry to his name!

D. S. *Now to my heart is the blood ap-plied, Glo-ry to his name!*

CHORUS.

Glo-ry to his name! Glo-ry to his name! Glo-ry to his name! Glo-ry to his name!

No. 233.

1 I hear the Saviour say,
Thy strength indeed is small,
Child of weakness, watch and pray:
Find in me thine all in all.

CHO.—Jesus paid it all!
All to Him I owe;
Sin had left a crimson stain:
He washed it white as snow.

2 For nothing good have I
Whereby Thy grace to claim;
I'll wash my garment white
In the blood of Calvary's Lamb.

3 When from my dying bed
My ransomed soul shall rise,
Then "Jesus paid it all!"
Shall rend the vaulted skies.

4 And when before the throne
I stand in Him complete,
I'll lay my trophies down,—
All down at Jesus' feet.

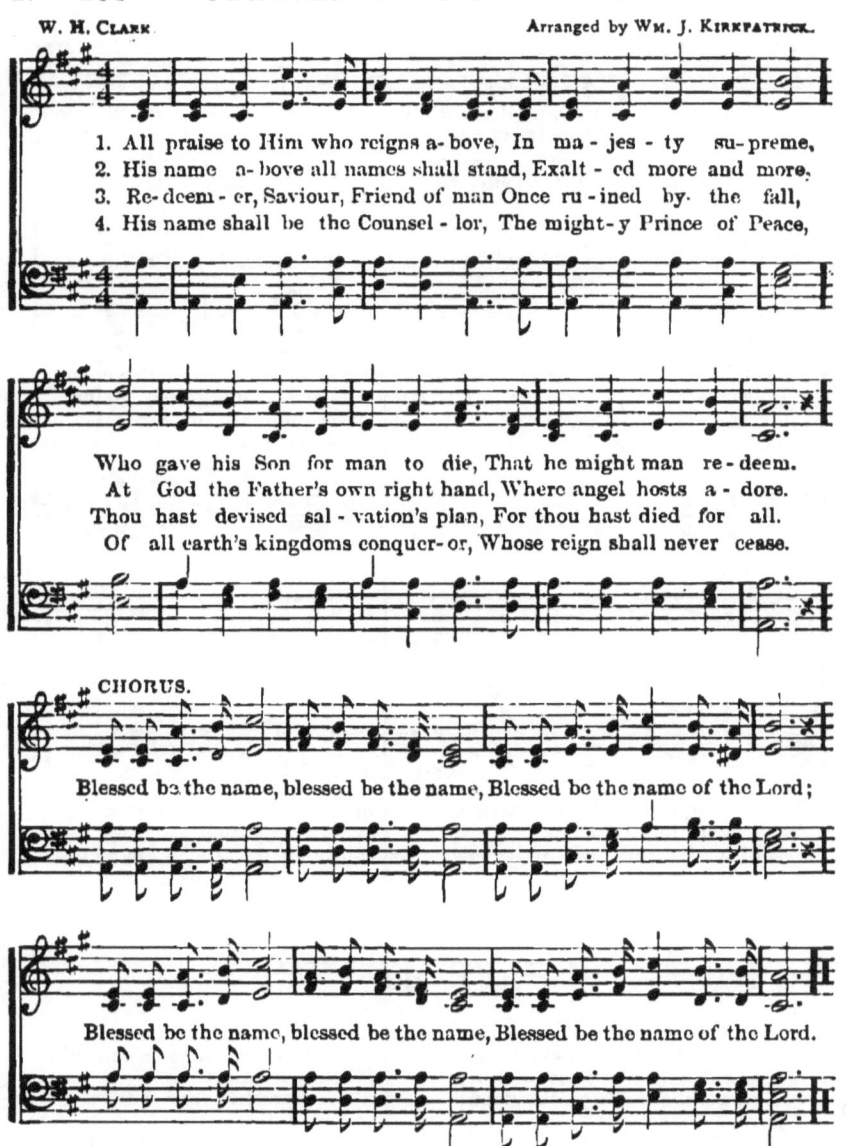

5 The ransomed hosts to thee shall bring
   Their praise and homage meet;
   With rapturous awe adore their King,
   And worship at his feet.

6 Then shall we know as we are known,
   And in that world above
   Forever sing around the throne
   His everlasting love.

No. 239. GLORIOUS FOUNTAIN.

COWPER.   T. C. O'KANE.

1. There is a fountain filled with blood, filled with blood, filled with blood, And sinners, plung'd beneath that flood, beneath that flood, beneath that flood,
2. The dying thief rejoiced to see, rejoiced to see, rejoiced to see, And there may I, tho' vile as he, tho' vile as he, tho' vile as he,

There is a fountain filled with blood, Drawn from Immanuel's veins,
And sinners, plung'd beneath that flood, Lose all their guilty stains.
The dying thief rejoiced to see That fountain in his day,
And there may I, tho' vile as he, Wash all my sins away.

CHORUS.

Oh, glorious fountain! Here will I stay, And in thee ever Wash my sins away.

3 Thou dying Lamb. ‖: Thy precious blood, :‖
Shall never lose its power,
Till all the ransomed ‖: Church of God, :‖
Are saved to sin no more.

4 E'er since by faith ‖: I saw the stream, :‖
Thy flowing wounds supply,
Redeeming love ‖: love, has been my theme, :‖
And shall be till I die.

No. 240. I GAVE MY LIFE.

1 I gave my life for thee,
  My precious blood I shed,
That thou might'st ransom'd be,
  And quickened from the dead;
I gave, I gave my for thee,
  What hast thou given for me?

2 My Father's house of light—
  My glory circled throne
I left, for earthly night,
  For wand'rings sad and alone;
I left, I left it all for thee;
  Has thou left aught for me?

3 I suffered much for thee,
  More than thy tongue can tell,
Of bitterest agony,
  To rescue thee from hell;
I've borne, I've borne it all for thee,
  What hast thou borne for me?

4 And I have brought to thee,
  Down from my home above,
Salvation full and free,
  My pardon and my love;
I bring, I bring rich gifts to thee,
  What hast thou brought to me?

There's a Heaven in the Heart. Concluded.

No. 247. LORD REVIVE US.

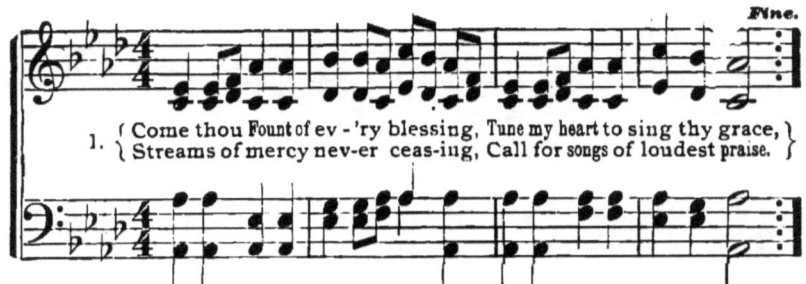

1. Come thou Fount of ev-'ry blessing, Tune my heart to sing thy grace,
Streams of mercy nev-er ceas-ing, Call for songs of loudest praise.

D. C. Lord revive us, oh, revive us, All our help must come from thee.

CHORUS.

Lord revive us, oh, revive us, All our help must come from thee.

2 Teach me some melodious sonnet,
Sung by flaming tongues above;
Praise the mount, I'm fixed upon it,—
Mount of thy redeeming love.

3 Here I'll raise mine Ebenezer,
Hither by thy help I'm come,
And I hope by thy good pleasure
Safely to arrive at home.

4 Jesus sought me when a stranger
Wandering from the fold of God;
He to rescue me from danger,
Interposed his precious blood.

5 Oh! to grace how great a debtor
Daily I'm constrained to be;
Let thy goodness, like a fetter,
Bind me closer, Lord, to thee.

6 Prone to love thee, Lord, I feel it,
Prone to love thee and adore,
Here's my heart, oh, take and seal it,
Wholly thine forever more.

No. 248.

1 Come, ye sinners, poor and needy,
Weak and wounded, sick and sore,
Jesus ready stands to save you,
Full of pity, love and power,
‖: He is able, he is able,
He is willing, doubt no more. :‖

2 Come, ye thirsty, come and welcome;
God's free bounty glorify;
True belief and true repentance,
Every grace that brings us nigh—
‖: Without money, without money,
Come to Jesus Christ and buy. :‖

3 Come, ye weary, heavy laden,
Lost and ruined by the fall;
If you tarry till you're better,
You will never come at all:
‖: Not the righteous, not the righteous,
Sinners, Jesus came to call. :‖

4 Let not conscience make you linger,
Nor of fitness fondly dream;
All the fitness he requireth
Is to feel your need of him:
‖: This he gives you, this he gives you,
'Tis the Spirit's rising beam. :‖

No. 250. I Have It in My Soul, Hallelujah!

Dedicated to my friend William P. Pratt, Portland, Maine.

E. S. U.   Rev. E. S. UFFORD.

1. Come weep just as we did in sorrow for sin, Come knock till the Lord bid you en-ter within; Come trusting, expect-ing, there's no other way, And soon you will find it the gladsome new day.
2. Come pray just as we did to live hour by hour, Above earth's temptations with God's keeping pow'r; To kneel oft in pray-er is vic-t'ry be-gun, Thus wrestling with evil the crown will be won.
3. Come shout just as we did your "Glory to God!" Sing praises to Je-sus who saves by His blood; The song of re-demption shall be our refrain Till in the new heaven we sing it a-gain.

CHORUS.

I have it in my soul, hal-le-lu-jah! I have found the Saviour precious all the way; I was once a child of sin, but I let my Saviour in, And there's sunlight in my soul to-day.

Copyright, 1894, by Rev. E. S. Ufford.

No. 251. ALL TAKEN AWAY.

R. KELSO CARTER, except 1st verse.

1. Did you hear what Jesus said to me? They're all taken a-way, away,
2. Oh, this wondrous grace so full and free; They're all taken a-way, away.
3. Now the cleansing streams of mercy flow; They're all taken a-way, away,
4. I have plunged beneath the crimson tide; They're all taken a-way, away,

Your sins are pardoned and you are free, They're all taken a - way.
Tho' red like crimson, they're now as wool; They're all taken a - way.
My sins like scar-let are white as snow; They're all taken a - way.
And now by faith I am pu - ri - fied; They're all taken a - way.

CHORUS

They're all tak-en a-way, a-way, They're all taken away, a-way,

They're all tak-en a-way, a-way, My sins are all tak-en a-way.

Copyright, 1891, by R. Kelso Carter. Used by per.

5 Oh, the cleansing blood has washed my soul,
   They're all taken away, away;
And Jesus' healing has made me whole;
   They're all taken away.

6 Now the Spirit witnesses to me;
   They're all taken away, away;
And keeps me standing in liberty;
   They're all taken away.

7 So I praise the Lord for sins forgiven,
   They're all taken away, away;
While onward pressing my way to heav'n;
   They're all taken away.

8 And when in glory we meet above;
   They're all taken away, away;
We'll sing the song of Redeeming Love;
   They're all taken away.

No. 252. IS NOT THIS THE LAND BEULAH.

Anon. Arranged.

1. I am dwelling on the mountain, Where the gold-en sunlight gleams
2. I can see far down the mountain, Where I wandered wea-ry years,
3. I am drinking at the foun-tain, Where I ev - er would a-bide;

O'er a land whose wondrous beauty Far ex-ceeds my fond-est dreams;
Oft-en hindered in my journey By the ghosts of doubts and fears,
For I've tast-ed life's pure riv-er, And my soul is sat-is-fied;

Where the air is pure, e-the-real, La-den with the breath of flowers,
Bro-ken vows and disappointments Thick-ly sprinkled all the way,
There's no thirsting for life's pleasures, Nor a-dorn-ing, rich and gay,

CHO.—*Is not this the land of Beu-lah? Bless-ed, bless-ed land of light,*

D. S. CHORUS.

They are blooming by the fountain, 'Neath the am - a - ran-thine bow's.
But the Spir-it led, un-err-ing, To the land I hold to-day.
For I've found a rich-er treas-ure, One that fad-eth not a-way.

Where the flow-ers bloom forev-er, And the sun is al-ways bright.

4 Tell me not of heavy crosses,
Nor the burdens hard to bear,
For I've found this great salvation
Makes each burden light appear;
And I love to follow Jesus,
Gladly counting all but dross,
Worldly honors all forsaking
For the glory of the Cross.

5 Oh, the Cross has wondrous glory!
Oft I've proved this to be true;
When I'm in the way so narrow,
I can see a pathway through;
And how sweetly Jesus whispers:
Take the Cross, thou need'st not fear,
For I've tried the way before thee,
And the glory lingers near.

No. 254. JESUS SAVES ME.

G. R. STUART   ZOLLIE STUART

1. Jesus, my all, to heav'n is gone, Glory hallelujah, Jesus saves me;
2. This is the way I long have sought, Glory hallelujah, Jesus saves me;
3. The King's highway of holiness, Glory hallelujah, Jesus saves me;
4. My grief a burden long has been, Glory hallelujah, Jesus saves me;
5. Lo! glad I come; and Thou, blest Lamb, Glory hallelujah, Jesus saves me;
6. Nothing but sin have I to give; Glory hallelujah, Jesus saves me;
7. Then will I tell to sinners 'round, Glory hallelujah, Jesus saves me;

He whom I fix my hopes upon; Glory hallelujah, Jesus saves me.
And mourned because I found it not; Glory hallelujah, Jesus saves me.
I'll go, for all His paths are peace, Glory hallelujah, Jesus saves me.
Because I was not saved from sin, Glory hallelujah, Jesus saves me.
Shalt take me to Thee, as I am; Glory hallelujah, Jesus saves me.
Nothing but love shall I receive, Glory hallelujah, Jesus saves me.
What a dear Saviour I have found, Glory hallelujah, Jesus saves me.

He saves me, He saves me, Glo-ry hal-le-lu-jah, Jesus saves me.
Hal-le-lu-jah, Hal-le-lu-jah,

Copyright, 1896, by Charlie D. Tillman.

No. 255. I BELIEVE JESUS SAVES.

Tune "Sweet Bye and Bye."

1 I am coming to Jesus for rest,
    Rest, such as the purified know;
   My soul is athirst to be blest,
    To be washed and made whiter than snow.

Cho. I believe Jesus saves,
    And His blood washes whiter than snow,
   I believe Jesus saves,
    And His blood washes whiter than snow.

2 In coming, my soul I deplore,
    My weakness and poverty show;
   I long to be saved evermore,
    To be washed and made whiter than snow.

3 To Jesus I give up my all,
    Ev'ry treasure and idol I know;
   For His fullness of blessing I call,
    Till His blood washes whiter than snow.

4 I am trusting in Jesus alone,
    Trusting now His salvation to know;
   And His blood doth so fully atone,
    I am washed and made whiter than snow.

5 My heart is in raptures of love,
    Love, such as the ransomed ones know,
   I am strengthened with might from above,
    I am washed and made whiter than snow.

Rev. WM. McDONALD.

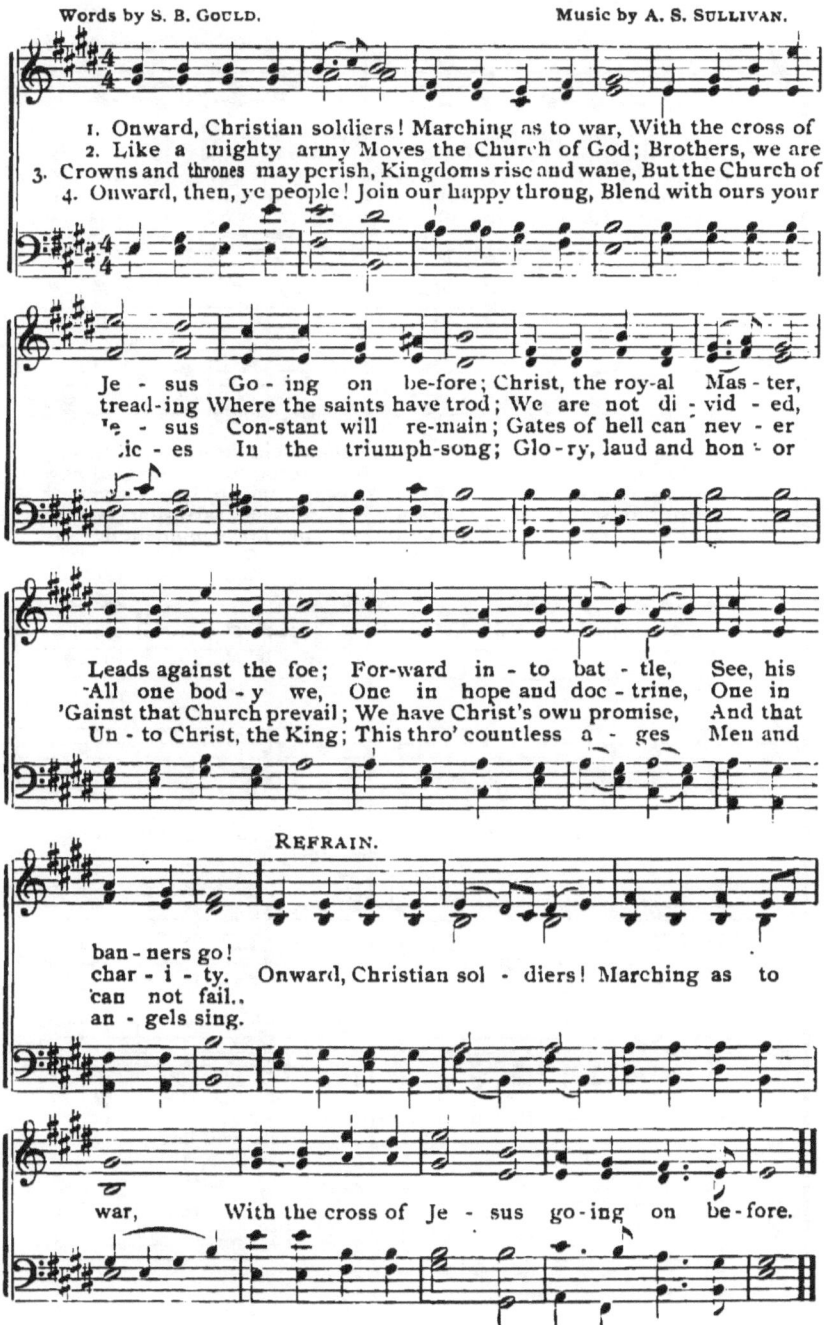

JESUS IS WAITING TO SAVE. Concluded.

Him now, come to Him now, Je-sus is wait-ing to save.
save you now.

No. 258. COME, COME TO THE SAVIOUR.

A D. FILLMORE.   J. H. FILLMORE.

1. Come, come to the Sav-iour, Rich mer-cy re-ceive;
2. Come, la-den and wea-ry, Christ calls thee to come;
3. Come, seek His sal-va-tion, Now hear and o-bey;
4. Hark! an-gels are sing-ing, Love, love is their theme;

Here you will find par-don, Je-sus from sin will re-lieve.
Leave paths dark and drea-ry, Cease from the Sav-iour to roam.
Hark! the sweet in-vi-ta-tion, An-gels in-vite you a-way.
Peace joy-ful-ly bring-ing, Mer-cy from God the Su-preme.

REFRAIN.

Come, come, come, come, Come to the Sav-iour and live;
Come, come, come, come, Je-sus will guide thee safe home;
Come, come, come, come, Sin-ner, be-lieve and o-bey;
Come, come, come, come, Je-sus is rich to re-deem.

Come, come, come, come, Come to the Sav-iour and live.
Come, come, come, come, Je-sus will guide thee safe home.
Come, come, come, come, Sin-ner, be-lieve and o-bey.
Come, come, come, come, Je-sus is rich to re-deem.

Copyright, 1896, by Fillmore Bros.

No. 263. MORE ABOUT JESUS.

E. E. Hewitt. Jno. R. Sweney.

1. More about Je-sus would I know, More of his grace to oth-ers show;
2. More about Je-sus let me learn, More of his ho-ly will dis-cern;
3. More about Je-sus; in his word, Holding communion with my Lord;
4. More about Je-sus; on his throne, Riches in glo-ry all his own;

More of his sav-ing full-ness see, More of his love who died for me.
Spir-it of God, my teach-er be, Showing the things of Christ to me.
Hearing his voice in ev-'ry line, Making each faith-ful say-ing mine.
More of his kingdom's sure increase; More of his coming, Prince of Peace.

REFRAIN.

More, more a-bout Je-sus, More, more a-bout Je-sus;

More of his sav-ing full-ness see, More of his love who died for me.

COPYRIGHT, 1887, BY JNO. R. SWENEY. BY PER.

No. 271. THE FOUNTAIN.

ZECH. 13 : 1.
To our Friend and Brother, Rev. Earnest Robinson.

Rev. LEONIDAS ROBINSON. EDW S. FOGG

The first 8 measures, or Bass Solo may be omitted if desired

CHORUS

1. There is a fountain flow-ing free, With bright and crim-son sheen; 'Twas opened in King David's time, To save and cleanse from sin.
2. On Calvary's brow the Saviour bled, For you His life He gave; He bore the sins of all the world, And from all sins doth save. This fountain opened in David's time, in Dav-id's time, Flows for all mankind, for all mankind, Who-so-ev-er will en-ter in, will enter in, saved and cleansed from sin, and cleansed from sin. This fountain opened in David's time, Still flows for all mankind, And
3. Come, sinner, come, your sins confess, And let this fountain roll; With cleansing pow'r the crim-son tide Will wash and make you whole.
4. I come, O Lord, with con-trite heart, I all my sins for-sake; I plead Thy promise, trust Thy word, I now my Saviour take.

time, Still And time, in David's time, kind, for all mankind,
in, Shall be sin, opened in David's time, Still flows for all mankind, And

Copyright, 1896, by Fogg & Barker.

Some Mother's Child. Concluded.

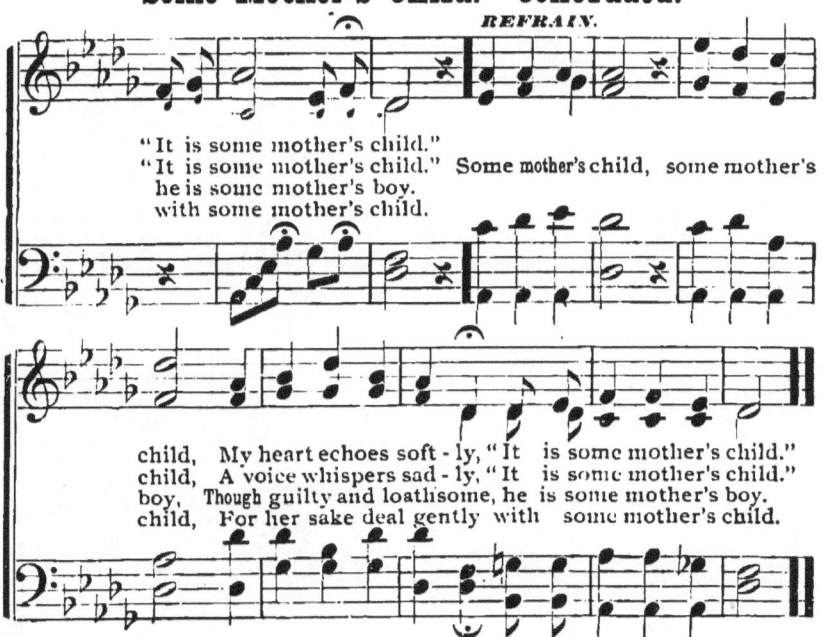

"It is some mother's child."
"It is some mother's child." Some mother's child, some mother's
he is some mother's boy.
with some mother's child.

child, My heart echoes soft-ly, "It is some mother's child."
child, A voice whispers sad-ly, "It is some mother's child."
boy, Though guilty and loathsome, he is some mother's boy.
child, For her sake deal gently with some mother's child.

No. 274. Look on the Cross.

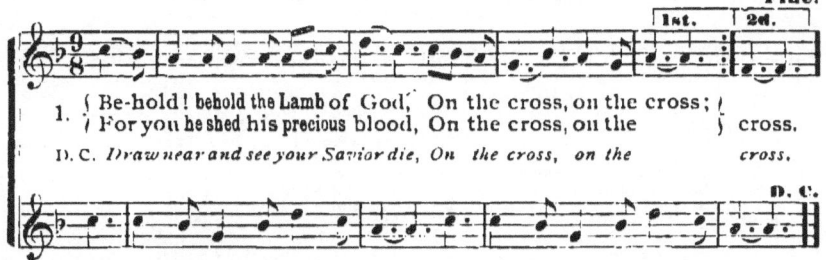

1. Be-hold! behold the Lamb of God, On the cross, on the cross;
   For you he shed his precious blood, On the cross, on the cross.
   D.C. Draw near and see your Savior die, On the cross, on the cross.

Now hear his ag-o-niz-ing cry, "E-loi-la-ma sa-bac-tha-ni."

2 Come, sinners, see him lifted up,
  On the cross, on the cross;
He drinks for you the bitter cup,
  On the cross, on the cross.
To heaven he turns his languid eyes,
"'Tis finished," now the Conqueror cries,
Then bows his sacred head and dies,
  On the cross, on the cross.

3 'Tis done! the mighty deed is done,
  On the cross, on the cross;
The battle fought, the victory won,
  On the cross, on the cross.

The rocks do rend, the mountains quake,
While Jesus doth atonement make,
While Jesus suffers for your sake,
  On the cross, on the cross.

4 Where'er I go I'll tell the story
  Of the cross, of the cross;
In nothing else my soul shall glory,
  Save the cross, save the cross.
Yes, this my constant theme shall be,
Through time and in eternity,
That Jesus suffered death for me,
  On the cross, on the cross.

INDEX.

Title	No.
Abiding and Confiding	168
Again we Have Come	235
Ah, Many Hearts are Aching	27
Alas, and did my Saviour Bleed	86
All Hail the Power of Jesus' Name	112
All Things are Ready	55
All taken Away	251
All the World for Jesus	186
All praise to Him	238
A little Talk with Jesus	41
A little Child is Kneeling	155
Am I a Soldier of the Cross?	103
Amazing Grace	146
America	125
Antioch	117
And must I be to Judgment Brought?	109
Anywhere He wants me	220
A Mother's Plea	189
Are you Watching?	43
Are you Walking with the Lord?	111
Arise, my Soul	121
At the Cross	86
At the Fountain	81
Autumn	134
Beautiful Beckoning Hands	175
Beautiful Pool	188
Beyond the Grave	124
Blessed Assurance	48
Blessed be the Name	238
Blessed be the Tie	50
Blow ye the Trumpet	122
Brave Little Soldiers	70
Brighter and Brighter	15
Bringing in the Sheaves	184
Bring Them in	218
Brother, Hear the Invitation	191
Calvary's Stream is Flowing	178
Calvary	179
Calling the Prodigal	202
Can a Boy Forget his Mother?	242
Children's Song	69
Christ is All	104
Christ our Redeemer	72
City of Gold	36
Come to the Feast	55
Come, Holy Spirit	144
Come, Every Soul	217
Come, Sinners, to the Gospel Feast	74
Come, Thou Fount of Every Blessing	247
Come to the Saviour (Second No. 90)	90
Come, come to the Saviour	258
Come, Weep just as we Did	250
Come, ye Sinners	248
Come, ye Epworth Band	231
Convert's Praises	96
Coronation	112
Dark and Stormy is the Desert	46
Dare to be a Paul	98
Dear Friend, if to-night, midst	189
Deliverance will Come	154
Diamonds in the Rough	27
Did you Hear What Jesus said to me?	251
Don't you Want to be There?	166
Down at Calvary's Fountain	16
Down at the Cross	232
Down at the Saviour's Feet	139
Down in the Licensed Saloon	243
Do you Fear the Foe?	198
Do you Hear the voice?	44
Enough for Me	95
Entire Consecration	261
Ever be Faithful	3
Every Hour I need Thy Blessing	226
Farther On	46
Father, I Stretch my Hands to Thee	201
Fear not Thou Careworn One	160
Fill me Now	24
For all the Lord has Done for Me	265
For God and Home and Native Land	211
For Me	272
Forward Leaguers	231
From Egypt's Cruel Bondage	221
From that Dear Cross	178
Full Salvation	199
Gentle Shepherd, Keep us in Thy Fold	20
Glory to God, I am at the Fountain	81
Glory to His Name	232
Glory to Jesus	90
Glorious Fountain	239
God be With You	266
God is Calling	262
Going Home	149
Go Wash in That Beautiful Pool	188
Go Ye into all the World	171
Gracious Spirit, Love Divine	115
Guide	122
Hallelujah	52
Hark, the Herald Angels Sing	64
Hark, the Master Calls for Reapers	92
Hark, the voice, Jesus crying	137
Hark, 'tis the Shepherd's Voice I Hear	218
Have you Ever Heard the Story?	172
Have you on the Wedding Garment?	11
He Came to Save me	62
Heaven in the Heart	246
Healed Pinion	17
Hear the Gentle Spirit's Call	88
He is Able to Deliver Thee	222
He Maketh the Storm a Calm	34
He Saves	17
He Waits for Thee	
His Yoke is Easy	60
Holy Ghost with Light Divine	116
Holy Spirit, Faithful Guide	130
Hover o'er me, Holy Spirit	24
How I Love Jesus	68
How Firm a Foundation	205
How I Love Thee	148
How Sweet the Name of Jesus Sounds	131
I Heard my Loving Saviour Say	165
I am Coming to the Cross	188
I am Coming to Jesus for Rest	255
I am Dwelling on the Mountain	252
I am Going to a City	63
I am Happy in the Lord	260
I am Glad I ever Heard the Blessed	130

	No.		No.
I am Resolved to Linger no Longer.	23	Lenox	118
I am the Lord's	194	Let the Sunshine in	198
I am now a Child of God	29	Life's Railway to Heaven	200
I am the Vine	195	Lift me Higher	170
I am Satisfied	208	Linger no Longer	23
I believe Jesus Saves	255	Little Soldiers	70
I can Join the Convert's Praises	96	Little Hands to Work	69
I Could not do Without Thee	83	Look not Far Away, my Brother	246
I do Believe	201	Lord, I am Thine	141
I Dreamed that the Great Judgment	4	Lord, Revive us	247
I Entered once a Home of Care	104	Lost, Lost on the Mountains	99
If we knew when Walking Thoughtless.	236	Lost After all	155
If you Want Pardon	90	Love Divine	142
I Save my Life for Thee	240	**Love Found me**	2
I Have Been to Jesus	58	**Look** on the Cross	274
I have it in my Soul	250	Marching to Victory	13
I Have Been Saved from the Power	31	Marching to the Land Above	40
I Have Learned the Wondrous Secret	168	Martyn	215
I Have Seen a Mother Weeping	234	Mighty Army of the Young	185
I Have Heard my Saviour Calling	181	More About Jesus	263
I Have Something Jesus gave me	80	Moving Toward the City	42
I Have Work Enough to do	30	Must Jesus Bear the Cross Alone?	143
I Hear the Saviour say	233	My Country, 'tis of Thee	129
I Know not why God's Wondrous	21	My Faith Looks up to Thee	128
I Know I Love Thee Better, Lord	237	My Feet are on the Highway	82
I Know my Name is There	91	My Heavenly Home	152
I Learned the Precious Secret	167	My Hope is Built on Nothing Less	209
I'll be There to Vote	211	My Mother's Bible	75
I'll go With Him	181	My Mother's Hands	245
I'm Believing and Receiving	147	My Name is in the Book of Life	91
I'm Going Home	152		
I'm Redeemed and Washed from Sin	16	Naught Have I to Make my Plea	187
I'm Satisfied with Jesus here	180	Nearer, my God, to Thee	161
In a World Where Sorrow ever will	7	Nothing but the Blood of Jesus	228
In the Awful Age of Night	67		
In the Days Long Gone by	124	Oh, Blessed Fellowship Divine	108
In the Resurrection Morning	176	Oh, do not Let the Word Depart	216
I now am Running in the Christian's	87	Oh, for a Thousand Tongues to Sing	100
I now Have the Spirit	52	Oh, for a Heart to Praise my God	102
I Never will Cease to Love Him	265	Oh, for a Faith	132
I Only Know it Reaches me	21	Oh, for a Closer Walk with God	133
I Saw a Happy Pilgrim	154	Oh, Fainting Soul by Sin Oppressed	224
I Stand all Bewildered with Wonder	156	Oh, Glorious Fountain	239
I Stood Outside the Gate	6	Oh, How I Love Jesus	68
Is not This the Land of Beulah?	252	Oh, Love, Surpassing Knowledge	95
It Reaches me	21	Oh, Land of Rest, for Thee I Sigh	157
It was Only a Drunkard	10	Oh, let the Current in	22
I've Been Washed in the Blood	58	Oh, Who can Forget the Kind Care?	97
I've Found the Pearl of Greatest Price	180	Oh, Mourner in Zion	203
I Want to be a Worker for the Lord	244	Oh, so Often we are Weary	173
I will Shout His Praise in Glory	18	Oh, Thou God of my Salvation	174
		Oh, Those Beautiful, Beautiful Hands	245
Jesus, Saviour, Pilot me	66	Old-time Power	1
Jesus, my Lord, to Thee I cry	19	Old-time Religion	182
Jesus Saves me	254	One Narrow Way	85
Jesus, the Light of the World	64	Once for All	54
Jesus is Pleading for Thee	88	Once I Wandered	219
Jesus Commands us to Forgive	145	Once I Wished	169
Jesus Lives	185	Only a Drunkard	10
Jesus Will Save	191	On the Hills Beyond	53
Jesus is Willing and Able to Save	192	Onward, Christian Soldiers	256
Jesus is Calling (Second No. 90)	90	Ortonville	126
Jesus, I my Cross Have Taken	213	Over Sin's Mountain	164
Jesus is Waiting to Save	257		
Jesus, Lover of my Soul	214	Pleyel's Hymn	114
Jesus, my All, to Heaven is Gone	254	Praise Him, Hallelujah	167
Jesus Paid it all	233	Praise His Name	165
Joy to the World	120	Praise for her Boy	97
Just as I Am	140	Precious Jesus, How I Love Thee	148
Just the Same To-day	172	Precious is the Blood	187
		Precious Saviour, Thou Hast Saved me	199
Keep Close to Jesus	71	Room at the Fountain	165
Keep us in Thy Fold	20	Rally Round the Cross	235
Knowing	169	Rejoice, Little Ones	49
		Rescue the Perishing	227
Land Ahead	37	Revive Thy Work	163
Lead me, Saviour, Lest I Stray	225	Revive us Again	153
Leaning on the Everlasting Arms	162	Rock of Ages	138
Leave it to Him	34	Rockingham	119

	No.
Safe Within the Vail	87
Salvation, Oh, the Joyful Sound	101
Saul's Journey to Damascus	45
Satisfied With Jesus	208
Saviour, Hear me	202
Saviour, Lead me, Lest I Stray	225
Saviour, Wash me in the Blood	249
Say, Where are you Going, my Brother?	8
Scatter Sunshine	7
Scattering Precious Seed	61
See the Lonely Prisoner	98
See, Jesus, Thy Disciples, see	110
Shall I Meet my Sainted Mother?	269
Shall I Turn Back?	99
Shall we Gather at the River?	25
Sinners, Turn, why Will ye Die?	79
Sins of Years are Washed Away	147
Since to my heart Jesus Came	31
Sitting at the Feet of Jesus	158
Something Jesus Gave me	80
Sometime, Somewhere	12
Sowing in the Morning	184
Sowing the Tares	59
Speak Gently to the Erring One	270
Speak Just a Word	73
Spread the Tidings	267
Standing on the Promises	223
Stand up, Stand up for Jesus	105
Steer Straight to the Light House	8
Step in the Life-boat	89
Step Out on the Promise	203
Sunshine in the Soul	207
Sweeping Through the Gates	29
Sweet Hour of Prayer	204
Sweet Peace the Gift of God's Love	241
Some Mother's Child	273
Take Me as I Am	19
Take My Life and Let it Be	261
The Coming Day	109
The Dispensation Day	67
The Fountain	271
The Gospel Feast	74
The Gates of Light Shall Open	160
The Half has Never yet Been Told	237
The Judgment	4
The Life-boat	78
The Life-boat is Launched	89
The Loyal Army	113
The Light of the Word Shines Brighter	15
The Last Chance	44
The Masters Calls for Reapers	92
The Music of His Name	94
The Morning Light is Breaking	106
The New Camp Ground	84
The New Song	177
The Penitent's Plea	202
The Resurrection	176
There is a Great Day Coming	253
There is a Fountain Flowing Free	271
There's a Hill, Lone and Gray	179
There's a Time That is Coming	210
There's a Song of a Broken Pinion	17
There's a City That Looks	36
There's a Dear and Precious Book	75
There is a Fountain	188, 229, 239, 249
There's an Open Fountain at the Cross	33
The Saviour With me	268
The Sands Have Been Washed in the	28
The Saviour is the Sinner's Friend	65
The Solid Rock	209

	No.
The Spirit is Calling	196
There's Sunshine in the Soul	207
Throw out the Life-line	93
Though Dark the Night	41
'Tis the Grandest Theme	222
'Tis the Old time Religion	182
Toplady	135
Toiling Now, Resting Then	30
To the Cross	39
Trust on	47
'Twas Rum that Spoiled my Boy	234
Unanswered Yet	12
Unfurl the Temperance Banner	107
Upon the Great Highway	5
Vote as you Pray	210
Walking in Fair Beulah Land	260
Wait on the Lord	51
Wait a Little While	177
Waiting for His Coming	173
Wash me in the Blood	249
Weary, Heavy-laden, Come	224
We are Marching to Zion	264
We are Moving Toward the City	42
We are Floating Down the Stream	78
Wedding Garment	11
We Have met To-day	84
We'll Walk in the Light	64
We'll Work till Jesus Comes	157
We Praise Thee, O God	153
We're on the Way	221
We're Marching to the Land Above	40
We Shall Run and not be Weary	87
What Will it Matter Bye and Bye?	26
What a Friend we Have in Jesus?	76
What a Fellowship?	162
What can Wash Away my Sins?	228
When I Get to the End of the Way	28
When I see the Blood	72
When Out in Sin and Darkness Lost	2
When the Lord Shall Call	56
When the People of God Were	45
When the Roll is Called Up Yonder	196
When you Start for the Land	71
When Jesus laid His Crown Aside	62
Where He Leads me I Will Follow	181
Where is my Wandering Boy To-night?	243
Where is my Soul To-night?	259
While Life Prolongs This Precious	123
Whiter Than Snow	49
Why do you Linger in Darkness?	257
Why go Around With Troubled Soul?	34
Why I Love Jesus	57
Why not To-night?	216
Why Stand ye Idle?	32
Who can Sing the Wondrous Song?	94
Who may Come?	197
Witness for Christ	111
Would you Know Why I Love Jesus?	57
Wonderful Words	212
Wonderful is the Saviour	205
Woodworth	136
Working With Jesus	193
Work for the Night is Coming	77
You Ask What Makes me Happy	18

THE ARMSTRONG PRINTING CO.
Music Typographers and Press,
419 Elm St., Cincinnati, O.

SHEET MUSIC.

Papa's Late Train,	15c.
Diamonds in the Rough,	10c.
Who Cares for Father,	20c.
Wandering Girl,	15c.
Mamma Kissed Me in Dream,	10c.
Only a Brakeman,	25c.
Bottle and the Baby (with four other beautiful songs),	10c.
Remember the Orphans (with four others),	10c.
Little Empty Shoes,	20c.
When the Car Goes By,	20c.

LITTLE LIGHT SONGS
For Little People
BRIGHT, CATCHY SONGS
With Some Motion Songs.

IN MUSLIN ONLY. 10 cents.

IN HIS SERVICE
By REV. J. L. TILLMAN.

Striking Incidents of Evangelistic Work
In Rural Districts of Southern States.

Get this and see how one can be used to spread the Gospel.

BOUND IN MUSLIN, 25 CENTS.

LEARN TO READ MUSIC

By Getting a Copy of **SINGING MADE EASY,**

By Charlie D. Tillman and John R. Bryant.

Something in which music is simplified and put in reach of all desiring a knowledge of music. Only 15 cents by mail. Special prices to teachers.

—ORDER FROM—

CHARLIE D. TILLMAN,

Atlanta, Ga.   Cincinnati, O.   Kansas City, Mo.

PRICES.

Name of Book.	Binding.	By Mail. Copy. cents	By Mail. Dozen	By Express. Dozen.	By Express. Hundre
The Revival No. 1..	Board	30	$3 60	$3 00	$20 00
" " " ..	Manila	20	2 25	1 75	12 00
The Revival No. 2,	Board	30	3 60	3 00	23 00
No. 3, or No. 4....	Muslin	25	3 00	2 50	18 00
The Revival No. 4 in Full Cloth.....		35	3 75	3 25	25 00
No. 4, Red, under gold edges	Morocco	$1 00			
Full Morocco, name in gilt.	....	1 25	....	....	.....
11th Hour Songs....	Manila	12	1 40	1 20	10 00
Little Light for Little Folks...	Board	20	2 75	2 00	15 00
	Muslin	12	1 35	1 20	10 00
Singing Made Easy, with Exercises...	Paper	15	1 75	1 50	12 00
Revival Special	Manila	15	1 75	1 50	12 00
" "	Full Cloth	25	3 00	2 50	20 00

In quantities of 25 or more of either of the above book: benefit of the hundred price.

The Revival No. 4 is also issued in transpo Bꝑ Cornet and Clarionet—soprano and alto parts. Large pag bound in full cloth, **$1.00,** postpaid.

All of these books are published in both Round and Sh

Be careful to specify which you prefer; also the numbe whether, 1, 2 or 3. We do not publish any of the books co:

PICTURE PUZZLE BIB
FOR CHILDREN.

150 pages, 9½ x 7¼ inches, bound in heavy l weight 2 lbs., mailed to any address, post-paid fo dollar. Specimen pages free.

Address all orders for any of the above publications to

Charlie D. Tillmaı
PUBLISHER,

Atlanta, Ga.,   Cincinnati, Ohio,   Kansas

www.ingramcontent.com/pod-product-compliance
Lightning Source LLC
Chambersburg PA
CBHW031746230426
43669CB00007B/509